PAVLO TYCHYNA

THE COMPLETE EARLY POETRY COLLECTIONS

PAVLO TYCHYNA:
THE COMPLETE EARLY POETRY COLLECTIONS
2nd Edition

Translated with an introduction by Michael M. Naydan
and with a guest introduction by Viktor Neborak

Book cover and interior layout by Max Mendor

Publishers Maxim Hodak & Max Mendor

© 2017, Michael M. Naydan

© 2017, Glagoslav Publications, United Kingdom

Glagoslav Publications Ltd
88-90 Hatton Garden
EC1N 8PN London
United Kingdom

www.glagoslav.com

ISBN: 978-1-911414-20-9
ISBN: 978-1-911414-21-6

A catalogue record for this book is available from the British Library.

This book is in copyright. No part of this publication may be reproduced, stored in a retrieval system or transmitted in any form or by any means without the prior permission in writing of the publisher, nor be otherwise circulated in any form of binding
or cover other than that in which it is published without a similar condition, including this condition, being imposed
on the subsequent purchaser.

PAVLO TYCHYNA

THE COMPLETE EARLY POETRY COLLECTIONS

TRANSLATED BY MICHAEL M. NAYDAN

GLAGOSLAV PUBLICATIONS

PAVLO TYCHYNA

1891 – 1967

INTRODUCTION

Since Ukrainian literature from the 18th century on has stood in the shadow of the politically more powerful Russian culture, few Ukrainian writers have achieved the international renown of their Russian counterparts. Nikolai Gogol ("Hohol" in Ukrainian) and Taras Shevchenko best exemplify the two divergent paths that have been open to Ukrainian writers. Gogol chose to become assimilated into Russian culture and achieved international fame, while Shevchenko preferred to write almost exclusively in Ukrainian, which led to his becoming the national bard of his homeland with less of an international reputation than Gogol. Nonetheless, the West, to at least some degree, still has been aware of Shevchenko's stature since he always has been compared favorably to his Romantic contemporaries Adam Mickiewicz and Alexander Pushkin. Gogol, though, it must also be noted, wrote in prose (albeit a highly poetic prose), a genre much more accessible than poetry to the Western reader in translation.

The general neglect of Ukrainian writers in world literature partly is a result of tsarist and, during the Soviet period, Stalinist politics.[1] While Europe was recovering from the ravages of World War I, the newly formed Soviet Union was rebuilding from the war, revolution, and civil war. The free Ukrainian National Republic survived from 1918 to 1921. Rather than oppressively stifling the assimilated Ukrainian lands, Lenin and the Bolsheviks chose to harness the resurgent Ukrainian nationalism to their advantage in building a new Soviet state. The 1920s saw a great renewal of Ukrainian culture under Lenin's New Economic Policy. Besides economic reforms geared to resuscitate a devastated economy, the period allowed for the relatively unrestrained development of the Ukrainian language and literature. This era marked the beginning of the transformation of a relatively uneducated and primarily agrarian population to an educated urban one, with concomitant cultural

---

1   For a survey of the cultural politics of the early Soviet period of Ukrainian literature, see George S.N. Luckyj, *Literary Politics in the Soviet Ukraine: 1917-1934*, Revised and Updated (Durham: Duke U. Press, 1990).

development. The Ukrainian language was no longer banned in print as it was during tsarist times. A Ukrainian press flourished. A great amount of cultural activity took place, and numerous trend setters emerged in the arts, most notably the prose writers Mykola Khvylovy and Valerian Pidmohylny, the playwright Mykola Kulish, the filmmaker Alexander Dovzhenko, the theatrical director Les Kurbas with his experimental Berezil Theater, and a number of others. The twenties particularly marked the development of a highly innovative poetry in Ukrainian belle-lettres, spanning from the Neoclassicist verse of Maksym Rylsky to the highly intellectual poetry of Mykola Bazhan. Pavlo Tychyna entered this period first as a Symbolist who, like his Russian counterparts Blok and Soloviev, predicted the appearance of Divine Sophia after a bloody conflagration.

Once Tychyna saw the reality of the bloodshed of revolution and civil war, he rejected it as the destruction of human values. These varied Ukrainian artists and literati continued the spirit of experimentation that was formulated in the visual arts by such Kyiv-born artists as Casimir Malevich and Alexander Archipenko. This experimentation, of course, paralleled artistic advancements in Europe and Russia, championed by such figures as Pablo Picasso, George Braque, Paul Klee, and Vassily Kandinsky. But the experimentation in Soviet Ukraine was short lived. Following the death of Lenin, Stalin crushed the cultural revival. The émigré scholar Yuri Lavrinenko has aptly designated this period of the late twenties and thirties in Soviet Ukraine as the "executed renaissance." Stalin instituted a policy of Russification and brutally attacked the intelligentsia with arrests and executions. Then he proceeded to assault the agrarian population in the early 1930s with an artificially induced famine that killed over seven million peasants. The repercussions of the terror were felt throughout all of Soviet Ukrainian society, both in human and in cultural terms. The leader of the Ukrainian communist party Mykola Skrypnyk committed suicide as did Khvylovy. Pidmohylny, Kulish, and Kurbas were arrested and later died in Siberian labor camps. The few leading figures who survived were forced to compromise their principles and to acquiesce to the demands of the state. Tychyna was one who managed to survive, in part, by acquiescing.

Pavlo Tychyna (1891-1967) is acclaimed as one of the leading Ukrainian poets of the modern period. His name invariably surfaces along with

Mykola Bazhan, Maksym Rylsky, and Bohdan Ihor Antonych as the most brilliant Ukrainian poets of the twentieth century.[2] One critic assesses him as a "unique innovator in poetic expression" and "one of the most outstanding Ukrainian poets of this century."[3] Another considers him a "bold innovator, supreme master of his craft,...and a poet of the first magnitude."[4] Various sources prolifically attest to Tychyna's poetic ability. For example, the leading Russian literary reference work, the *Brief Literary Encyclopedia*, refers to the "mastery of the poet-innovator" Tychyna, whose verse exhibits "musicality, richness of rhythm, [and] an organic fusion of symbolic and impressionist poetic devices with the folk song."[5] The now somewhat dated *Biobibliographical Dictionary of Ukrainian Writers* from the 1960s contains a list of more than twenty-five pages of Soviet-period critical works on him. A twelve-volume Soviet collected works edition of Tychyna appeared in the 1980s. And the monographs, critical articles, and memoirs by Ukrainian writers and literary critics continue to be produced at a steady pace. An unexpurgated version of his early works finally was published in Kyiv in 1990. There can be no doubt of Tychyna's prominence in his native culture, yet little is known of this brilliant poet in the West. Tychyna's virtuosity and innovativeness should have brought him to the forefront of world literature in his time with his European contemporaries such as T.S. Eliot, Ezra Pound, Rainer Maria Rilke, Anna Akhmatova, and Federico Garcia Lorca. Yet few in the English-speaking world have been made aware of his talent and accomplishments. It is time for this situation to be at least partly rectified and for Tychyna to take his rightful place in the history of world

---

2   Antonych is currently available in several English translations. See Bohdan Ihor Antonych, *Square of Angels: Selected Poems*, Trans. Mark Rudman and Paul Nemser with Bohdan Boychuk (Ann Arbor: Ardis, 1977). See also Bohdan Ihor Antonych, *The Grand Harmony*, Trans. Michael M. Naydan (Lviv: Litopys Publishers, 2007) as well as *The Essential Poetry of Bohdan Ihor Antonych: Ecstasies and Elegies*, Trans. Michael M. Naydan (Bucknell University Press, 2010). For translations of the poetry of Rylsky see Maksym Rylsky, Trans. Michael M. Naydan, *Autumn Stars: Selected Poetry of Maksym Rylsky* (Lviv: Litopys Publishers, 2008).

3   *Penguin Companion to European Literature* (New York, 1969): 777.

4   C.H. Andrusyshen and Watson Kirkconnell, *The Ukrainian Poets* (Toronto, 1963): 315.

5   VII (Moscow, 1972): 705.

poetry. While poets in the western tradition are all-too-often treated as aesthetes who write for a limited intellectual audience, poets (even in the modern period) in the Slavic tradition are honored with great reverence. They are often venerated as prophets and spokespersons for an entire nation or people, and the poetic word is treated as sacred. Much of Tychyna's early poetry fits the prophetic modality.

Tychyna's *Instead of Sonnets and Octaves* (1920) has been a work that far transcended an audience of merely literary critics and other poets. It influenced succeeding generations of readers to re-evaluate the revolution. Tychyna is less ambiguous about the nature and effects of the revolution than his Russian counterpart Alexander Blok, the author of *The Twelve*: Tychyna damns the violent law of the beast and calls for a return to spiritual and cultural values. The revolution is not the kind of "music" that Blok perceives in his poem, but rather a means for destruction of the true spirit of music, of culture.

Besides extraordinary poetic virtuosity in technique, Tychyna's poetry expresses great philosophical depth and feeling. Tychyna introduced a new genre into Ukrainian poetry – the tragic lyric, based on elements of Ancient Greek verse. Tychyna's early work has had an enormous impact on the development of twentieth-century Ukrainian poetry, and his collections provide a microcosm of the cultural and historical events in Ukraine during the turbulent period of the 1917 revolution and its aftermath. One can observe the emotional impact of those times on Tychyna, who, in his poetry, strove to reconcile himself with the seemingly cosmic forces unleashed by the revolution. In this respect, he shares a distinct affinity with Blok. Tychyna's poetry spans the development from a neo-Skovorodian religious philosopher and proponent of "Clarinetism" in his early works, to a troubled panegyrist of the Soviet regime after the publication of his collection *Chernihiv* in 1931. Tychyna coined the term "Clarinetism" (Kliarnetyzm) to describe his verse: the term finds a partial counterpart in the Russian poet Mikhail Kuzmin's concept of *klarizm* (a sense of clarity and surface simplicity). Kuzmin rejected the density and opaqueness of Russian Symbolism in favor of a poetry grounded in a refreshingly simple and accessible style. Tychyna strove to create a poetry that fuses stylistic clarity with the pure and haunting sound of the clarinet. In light of Tychyna's musicality and close ties to the earth, the émigré poet Vasyl Barka has described Tychyna as a "tillerman's Orpheus" (khliborobs'kyi Orfei), which fits aptly. John Fizer has also noted Tychyna's close affinity with Walt Whitman's cosmism, particularly in the collection *In the Orchestra of the Cosmos*.[6] Tychyna surely had read Whitman in Kornei Chukovsky's Russian translation, which may have been a strong influence on Tychyna's shift to a more prosaic poetry in *Instead of Sonnets and Octaves* and in parts of *Wind from Ukraine* (1924).

Tychyna was saved from the grim fate of some two-thirds of the Ukrainian intellectual community in the 1930s by his acquiescence to Stalinist literary requirements. His burgeoning fame also aided considerably in his survival. Yet the spirit of the Christian philosopher-poet Hryhory Skovoroda followed him throughout his life, culminating in his never completed lifelong project – the book-length long poem *Skovoroda*. Tychyna's poetry provides a concise compendium of the history of Soviet

Ukrainian culture from the early idealism of the revolution to the Civil War and its aftermath. The poems give a sensitive glimpse into the milieu of Soviet Ukraine of the 1920s, which reflects the cultural renaissance that occurred during the period of Gorbachev's reforms as well as after Ukrainian independence in 1991. The translation of Tychyna's poetry poses a number of specific problems since cultural, literary, and historical references abound. Tychyna was a renaissance man who exhibited an expert knowledge of Russian and European literatures, as well as the literature of antiquity. In order better to understand Tychyna, first and foremost one should look at the philosophical sources from which Tychyna draws, most importantly the eighteenth-century Ukrainian philosopher Skovoroda. As a Christian nature poet and in a sense a "sun worshiper" (the sun being a symbol of the illuminating force of God), Skovoroda provided a partial source for the generating force and half the title of Tychyna's first published collection, *Clarinets of the Sun* (Soniashni kliarnety, 1918). The cover illustration to that volume, a sunflower, visually creates the image of a clarinet, thus creating a representation of the metaphorical fusion of sight and sound so prevalent in Tychyna's early work. Skovoroda, in his philosophy, divided the world into the macrocosmic and the microcosmic, the latter comprising the inner human world. At the center of the macrocosmic world lies the sun, the source of light and life. *Instead of Sonnets and Octaves* opens with that

---

6   "Cosmic Oneness in Whitman and Tychyna: Some Similarities and Differences." *Canadian Slavonic Papers* (June 1986): 149-156.

Skovorodian burst of solar energy and specifically incorporates elements of Skovoroda's "Nineteenth Song" from his *Garden of Divine Songs*.[7]

The translations here are based on the following edition: Pavlo Tychyna, *Soniachni klarnety: poezii* (Kyiv: Dnipro Publishers, 1990). This particular volume comprises the first completely unexpurgated edition of Tychyna's early works to be published in Ukraine since the original publications in the early part of the 20th century. I have decided to translate Tychyna's first five books in their entirety for this volume, since this marks Tychyna's most fertile lyrical period before he began to write in the government-imposed fashion of Socialist Realism. These collections include: *Soniashni klarnety* (*Clarinets of the Sun*, 1918), *Pluh* (*The Plow*, 1920), *Zamist' sonetiv i oktav* (*Instead of Sonnets and Octaves*, 1920), *V kosmichnomu orkestri* (*In the Orchestra of the Cosmos*, 1921), and *Viter z Ukrainy* (*Wind from Ukraine*, 1924). With the approaching 100-year anniversary of the Bolshevik Revolution of 1917 in 2017, it is important to note that Tychyna's early collections also largely comprise a lyrical diary of the tragic events of those times in Ukraine from the Revolution, to the Civil War, to consolidation of Soviet power in the early 1920s.

Linguistically, Tychyna's poetry causes many difficulties for the translator.

Influenced in part by Dadaism and the Futurists, especially in his early poetry, Tychyna makes extensive use of paronomasia. The titled segment of *Instead of Sonnets and Octaves* that I translate as "Rock-a," as part of the formulaic rock-a-bye *liuli-liuli*, provides a prime example. The Ukrainian original is *Liu*, which, besides being part of the locution suggesting a child's lullaby, is also the typical first person singular ending of Ukrainian verbs. It also forms the reduplicated component for the Ukrainian word *liubliu*, meaning "I love." Throughout this entire section of the poem Tychyna makes use of assonances and alliterations, playing on the sounds "l," "iu" and "o." The poem "Fornarina" provides another excellent illustration of Tychyna's paronomastic play: in it sounds take on meanings of their very own. This aspect of his poetry is sometimes lost in translation. I also strive to create equivalents in English for Tychyna's striking Ukrainian neologisms. I try to convey Tychyna's musicality

---

[7]   My translation of *The Garden of Divine Songs and Collected Poetry of Hryhory Skovoroda* appeared with Glagoslav Publishers in 2016.

whenever it can be done naturally in English, but for the full effect of this profound feature of his poetry, one should read him in the original.

I feel that certain of my translations are more successful in English than others, but I have published them in their entirety in order to maintain the integrity of the collections. By any measure these translations cannot even begin to convey the totality of Tychyna's talent. Some sound elements in the original texts are virtually untranslatable in English, so I have opted in favor of restraint over exactness in conveying the musicality and rhythm. I have toned down a bit of what critics have called Tychyna's "infantilism," a completely childlike vision of the world, since this is a feature less readily accessible to readers of English.

Since my initial bilingual edition of *The Complete Early Poetry Collections of Pavlo Tychyna* published by Litopys Publishers in 2000 has long been sold out, I have decided to publish this English-language expanded edition of Tychyna's early poetry to make his poetry accessible to a wider readership in the Anglophone world. For this expanded collection I have also decided to translate Tychyna's quite poignant longer poems "Mother was Peeling Potatoes" (1926) and "Funeral of My Friend" (1942) as well as his highly patriotic "In Memory of the Thirty" (1918), the latter of which was banned in Soviet times.

Michael M. Naydan,
Woskob Family Professor of Ukrainian Studies,
The Pennsylvania State University

ACKNOWLEDGMENTS

I owe my greatest debt to the National Endowment of the Humanities for a Translation Grant, which gave me a year's sabbatical from teaching to complete versions of all the translations presented here and to work on the scholarly apparatus for the volume. I am grateful to the Shevchenko Scientific Society in New York for a research grant to aid in my initial research on the Tychyna translation project. Extra special thanks to the Endowment for Ukrainian Studies, established by the Woskob family, at The Pennsylvania State University, which helped to make this volume a reality. I am grateful to Bohdan Boychuk and Vasyl Barka for assistance on my early work on Tychyna and for educating me on the art of his poetry. I am thankful to Oksana Zabuzhko for going over the first complete manuscript of my translations and for comparing them with the original texts. Thanks also to Mykola Riabchuk, Natalka Bilotserkivets, Viktor Neborak, John Fizer, Maria Zubrytska, and Oksana Tatsyak for sharing their expert knowledge of Tychyna with me, as well as to Lowry Nelson, Jr. for his commentary on *Instead of Sonnets and Octaves*. My gratitude to Christine Skolnick for editing suggestions on a more recent version of the manuscript, and to Christine Sochocky for her meticulous attention to detail on the final galleys and for some fine suggestions for final emendations.

I wish to thank Penn State's Pattee Library Interlibrary Loan Office for their kindness in acquiring copies of difficult to find materials. I also thank the following libraries for the courteous assistance of their staffs: Columbia University's Butler Library, Princeton University's Firestone Library, Harvard University's Houghton Library, the New York Public Library, the Library of Congress, and especially the U. of Illinois at Urbana Slavic Collection, whose summer research program granted me funding twice to work on this project.

Extra special thanks to Mykhailo Komarnytsky, Natalia Babalyk and to Myroslava Prykhoda for the attentive care they gave to the publication of the original Litopys Publishers bilingual edition of Tychyna in 2000. It could not have happened without them.

My gratitude to Vasyl Byalyk and Alla Perminova for assistance with resolving sticky wickets in the new translations for this volume – and to Svitlana Budzhak-Jones for her excellent suggestions that have made my translation of "Mother Was Pealing Potatoes" significantly better.

The poem "Along the Azure Steppe" first appeared in the literary journal Mr. Cogito. And the two introductions to this volume, the footnotes, and the translations of Tychyna's first five collections appeared originally in *The Complete Early Poetry Collections of Pavlo Tychyna* (Lviv: Litopys Publishers, 2000). Some translations have been slightly revised for this edition.

THE SENSES AND NONSENSES OF PAVLO TYCHYNA

For Professor Ivan Denysiuk

1.
Tychyna is the greatest poet of the *revolutionary* (modernist) twentieth century. And yet almost no one knows that.

2.
Right now almost no one reads Tychyna's books of poetry, not even his early ones, even though some Ukrainians still can quote a number of lines of poetry by him or one of the parodies of his poetry.

3.
For Pavlo Tychyna is also the greatest (anthologized) poet of the *Stalinist* empire. The right was given to him to "prompt" (in a rhymed voice) the new Soviet watchwords to the Father of Nations – Stalin. Tychyna's "feeling of a single family" is about a new society of people – at that time the international Soviet one, and now a democratic universal one.

4.
The Ukrainian rhythm of Tychyna's anthem *The Party Leads* coincided with *Let It Be* of the legendary *Beatles*. The famous Liverpoolers performed their anthem – more than thirty years after Tychyna's own Communist Party "debut" – in the rock-and-roll sixties, in the years when Tychyna the singer of youth was already an older man. Music is wavelike, and the waves of music ceaselessly traverse the matter of Time, modifying, layering one on top of the other.

5.
Tychyna listened to the Music of the Surrounding. More precisely – he listened to Music. It seemed that Tychyna did not differentiate

between the music within him and the music of the external world. The subject and object in him was a single whole.

6.
Music has turned into rhythm, rhythm – to noise, noise – into death, death – into the renewal of life and the human being. I dwell in music, therefore I exist – the Poet in our era of inexact (Post-Modernist) quotations might proclaim.

7.
Moreover, Tychyna is the most distinguished *Ukrainian* poet of the end of the Age of Pisces, a caller to and a harbinger of the Age of Clarinets of the Sun. To be a Ukrainian poet is to be hidden from the rest of the world, to be *inconspicuous*. What is *inconspicuous* in Tychyna coincides with his *Ukrainianness*. For almost everything Ukrainian is still inconspicuous in the eyes of the world.

8.
Everything that in Tychyna is Leninist and Stalinist is all too conspicuous. But the more things are conspicuous, the sooner they become boring. It seems that Tychyna all too well knew the price for this *overly conspicuous* level of things. But he couldn't avoid it as his favorite teacher Skovoroda did. Tychyna just adequately reflected these overly conspicuous things. It turns out that in Tychyna's versions of poetry the Leninist and Stalinist categories are not as horrifying as they are comic. The Stalinist censorship that was deaf to music – along with its entire investigative punitive apparatus – failed to notice this now obvious fact!

9.
Resistance to the Leninist-Stalinist Evil through non-violence was Tychyna's Christian choice. He *sacrificed* himself as a sunnyclarinetingly Ukrainian poet – and he preserved himself as a sunnyclarinetian. Writing from the "we" point of view instead of the "I" – here is the Stepping-in-Columns Spirit of the twentieth century fixed by Tychyna. Where Tychyna writes from the perspective of "we," false notes and primitive melodies appear. But "we" are not aware of it. Only the "I" can hear that falseness and primitiveness.

11.
"I was – not *I*..." (from the poem *Not Zeus or Pan*...). Perhaps the main question that the Sphinx of Time places before the poet is "who am I" with a capital letter? Perhaps might all the cataclysms, all the whirlwinds and all the plows of the twentieth century be just attempts to give an answer to this question?

12.
One way or another – melodies performed out of tune will not be listened to by those listeners who care about their musical ear. Ukrainians are divided by faith, by world view, by economics, by politics, by language. Perhaps musicality is the only thing that unifies Ukrainians today and is the only thing they have preserved in spite of all the world's dissonances-temptations. Thus the Music of Tychyna will resound and will purify all those capable of hearing it, and the false note consciously allowed by Tychyna will remain a grotesque witness of our cabaret-marching era.

Victor Neborak
June 7, 1999, Lviv
Translated by *Michael M. Naydan*

CLARINETS OF THE SUN
(1918)

NOT ZEUS, OR PAN, OR THE DOVE-SPIRIT...

Not Zeus, or Pan, or the Dove-Spirit
Just Clarinets of the Sun.
I am in a dance, a rhythmic movement,
In immortal dance – all the planets.

I was – not *I*. Just a thought, a dream.
All around are ringing sounds,
And the tunic of creative darkness
And blessed tiding hands.[8]

I awakened – and already I am You.
Above me, below me
Worlds glow, worlds run
Like a musical river.

And I watched, and springtimed:
The planets harmonized.
Forever I learned that You are not Wrath,
But only Clarinets of the Sun.

1918

---

8   *Blahovisni*, translated as "blessed tiding" here, suggests "Blahovishchennia" (the Annunciation).

THE CLOUDS SWIRLED INTO CURLS...

The clouds swirled into curls. Azure settled into the depth.
O, dear friend – my heart is ailing again –
O, dear brother – it's crucified again –
My ailing heart is whistling like a swan.[9]
The clouds swirled into curls...

The winds race stampeding![10] Poplars bend their harps...
Out of my soul – like lilies –
Growing beautiful – oh, so bright –
Out of my soul, regrets and sorrow grow like flowers.
The winds race stampeding!

The sun's mood is mirrored on lakes. Smoke weaves about the past...
I want to be – how can I forget?
Do I want – a dark-haired beauty[11] – again?
I want to be forever young, immutably young!
The sun's mood is mirrored on lakes.

Laughter, bells, and warm joy. A rainbow of thoughts blooms...
Sorrow clenches my heart: – the sun! a song! –
In my soul I set you out – I praise you! –
In my soul I set out a bright sail, for sadness is in my heart.
Laughter, bells, and warm joy.

1917

---

9   The European swan's whistling is often compared to the sound of a clarinet or trumpet, which may offer a link of the clarinet metaphor to the collection's title.
10 Literally: "like fierce aurochs."
11 Or: "a marigold."

GROVES RUSTLE

Groves rustle –
        I listen.
Clouds rush on –
        I feel delight.
I feel delight – I marvel at
    Why my soul
    Is so joyful.

A bell resounds
    From far away.
It spins thoughts
    As the fields sway.
Above the tides of fields,
    Bathing me
        like a swallow.

I walk and walk –
    Profoundly stirred.
Always waiting for someone –
    Singing.
Singing-loving
    To the rustle of the quiet whisper of grass
        caressing.

The grove can be seen[12]
    Above the river's sheen.
There the edge of sky far off
    Is like gold.
Like rolled, beaten gold
    The river glows and quivers
        like music.

1913

---

[12] A variant reading of this line could be: "The grove dreams of something."

LIKE HARPS, LIKE HARPS

Like harps, like harps –
the golden groves resounded
                        Selfstrumming:
         Spring is coming
              Fragrant,
       Adorned
                  With flower-pearls.
With thoughts, with thoughts –
The azure overflowed like the sea with ships
                        Tender-toned:
        There will be fiery
           Battle!
        There will be laughter, mother-of-pearl
           Lament.
I will stop and gaze about –
Rivulets everywhere like chimes, a golden lark
                     Undulating:
        Spring in full bloom
           Bountiful,
       Adorned
                With flower-pearls.
My love, my dearest –
Whether you walk forlorn, or filled with brimming happiness
                          There beyond the fields:
        O, open up
              The wheat husk of eyelashes[13]!

        There will be laughter, and mother-of-pearl
            Lament...
                             1914

---

13   Tychyna creates a visually realized metaphor here that does not translate well into English. He is comparing the appearance of a head of wheat with its delicate hair-like follicles and eye-like shape to an eye with eyelashes.

SOMEWHERE SPRING APPROACHED...

Somewhere spring approached. I told her: "You're spring!"
    Like gray-winged doves
    In the corners of her mouth
    Something flitted in smiles –
    And drowned in her soul...

The rye ripened. I told her: "You're golden!"
    Angrily her eyebrows splintered.
    She turned away. And left.
    And just kept looking back –
    As though she were calling out: "Come!"

The mists began to move. I said: "You don't love me!"
    She stopped. Looked. And spoke.
    Right then Autumn had just come.
    So, should I love? Tell me. Tell me right away!
    Her laughter flashed like a dagger...

The grove grew sullen beneath the snow. I said to her: then...
                                          good-bye!
    Suddenly with a warm and tender glow
    Something gushed from her eyes...
    Like a gray-winged dove
    She is on my lips!

1917

THE FLOWER IN MY HEART...

The flower in my heart,
A bright flower-primrose.[14]
You are that flower, my friend,
Silvery primrose.
Ah, again, my love,
Where the cut resonated,
The flower-primrose blooms!

I listen to the melodies
Of clouds, of lakes, of wind.
I strum, like the strings
Of the steppe, of the clouds, of the wind.
We all ring with our hearts,
We dream of red wine –
Of the sun, of clouds, of wind!

Somewhere there are fairy-tale lands,
And golden summits...
Only the path that leads
To those summits is thorny.
Stars pass and shine,
Waves undulate in the sea –
In rhythms to the summits!

Light is in my heart,
the dance of dreams and dawns.
You are that light, my friend,
A starry dawn.
I exalt your sparkling eyes,
Morning stars of the skies –
Like the dawning of the day!

1917

---

14   The word for primrose in Ukrainian literally means "the first flower."

DON'T LOOK SO FONDLY...

Don't look so fondly,
So apple-blossomy.
Stars ripen like wheat:
I'll feel sadness.

Don't caress me so silkily,
So bright-falconly.
At sunrise roses bloom:
Fair weather lies ahead.

At sunrise storms seethe –
Once again there will be tears!
Mother woke first, then father followed:
Where is she, our little swallow?

I'm here, in the garden, on a bench,
Among the marigolds...
What will I tell them? "All is so clear to me:
So apple-blossomy."

1918

SHE LOOKED AT ME BRIGHTLY...

She looked at me brightly – violins began to sing! –
She embraced me for the last time – in my soul. –
The forest was silent in sorrow, in black harmony,[15]
Violins began to sing in my soul!

I knew, I knew: forever that beams of light are like her lashes!
No longer will I see the sunny eyes.
I will be alone eternally, in black harmony.
Beams of light are like the lashes of her sunny eyes!

1918

---

15   Or: chord.

I CRIED FROM LOVE, I SOBBED...

I cried from love, I sobbed.
    (Above the copse clouds like a wall!)
Those tears rose between her and me –
    (Like a marble wall...)

Prayers float aloft.
    (Return with ringing laughter!)
A leaf falls on altars –
    (With a curly ringing...)

Somewhere snows have already fallen.
    (Above the copse clouds like a wall!)
And tender enemies are smashed –
    (By a marble wall...)

You're lonely, and I'm lonely.
    (Spring! – the dawn! – a cherry blossom!)
Your soul has shed its blossoms –
    (A cherry blossom flowered too soon...)

1917

O MISS INNA...[16]

O Miss Inna, darling Inna!
    I'm alone. A window. Snow...
I loved your sister once –
        In a childish golden glow.[17]
    Did I? – Long ago. Meadows had bloomed...
O Miss Inna, darling Inna!
The smile of love fleetingly blooms.
    Snow, more snow, more snow...

I remember your eyes.
    Like music, like a song.
A wintry evening. Silence. The two of us alone.
        I'm a stranger to you – I know.
    But someone shouts: you've met a kindred soul!
And suddenly – the sky... the whisper of the grove...
O no, these are Your eyes. – I sob.
    Is it your sister or you? – whom I loved...

                            1915

---

16   Tychyna has variant versions of the opening line that were written later for political purposes. The original version reads as follows: "O, panno Inno, panno Inno!" Tychyna uses the form "panna" (a pre-revolutionary form of address equivalent to the English "Miss") in the vocative case, obviously for its sound similarity to the girl's name Inna. After the Revolution and before Ukrainian independence, this particular form of address in Soviet Ukraine was not permitted. Inna was the nickname of Niusia Konoval, whose family Tychyna often frequented. Tychyna was infatuated with her sister Polina. Niusia's death in May 1920 deeply saddened him. I have been unable to reproduce Tychyna's extensive play on the double "n" consonantal sound of Inna's name in the original in English.

17   The adverbial form *zolototsinno* has its origin in the notion of selling concubines for their weight in gold.

I'M STANDING AT THE BEND...

I'm standing at the bend –
Beyond the river are bells:
I'm waiting for your sails –
A shadow sinks there somewhere...

Clouds swarm out –
Sorrow grows full like an ear of wheat:
Clouds becloud waves –
Sadly, I'm solitary, a shiny dream...

I believe starbrightly[18]
Across the river are bells:
I dream Taurus-like –
A shadow sinks there somewhere...

You'll float up, you'll come rushing –
Sorrow grows full like an ear of wheat:
With a song of the sun! –
Sadly, I'm solitary, a shiny dream.

1918

---

18   Literally Tychyna creates an adverbial neologism from the noun "omophorion," an eastern bishop's vestment draped over the shoulders. The western church equivalent is a pallium. Icons of the Mother of God often have her depicted with an omophorion, as an emblem of her as protectress. I am grateful to Oksana Tatsyak for suggesting the translation I use here from a different version of the poem that uses the word "iasnozorno."

THE POPLARS IN THE FALLOW FIELD ARE FREE...

The poplars in the fallow field are free
(Someone had brought a sacrifice at sundown)
And with the wind raging willful and wild,
They gracefully rush off somewhere into the sky...

I go into the open spaces, vigilant, with trepidation
(The day expires, dropping petals like a poppy).
There are tempests and thunderstorms in my heart,
And rumbling – the sobbing of *bandúra*[19] strings.

The wind bends the rye over the path
(Oh, there's a sullen storm cloud from the south).
And so sadly, so sadly it sings –
It's just a quail somewhere striking a bell...

My song, fiery and wild,
(It crumbles the sky and rolls its wrath),
Why don't you break into luminous chords.
Burst into sobs – and become silent as thunder...

1916

---

19   A Ukrainian folk instrument similar to the lute. It consists of some 30-66 strings and has a harp-like sound.

A GIRL'S EMBROIDERING...

A girl's embroidering and sobbing –
What fancy needlework!
With red and black threads she's embroidering
My life.

Sounds dance on the belfry,
And the bell sobs.
I go on. Sometimes my path is made of bits of straw,
Sometimes of dahlias.

Mists float up-up-up,
And clouds – down.
Why do I spurn the open spaces
When I'm dry-eyed?

In the evening I kiss the rose
And invoke sorrow.
Why, why is it I can't live alone
Without these thoughts?

1914

A FLOWERY MEADOW…

A flowery meadow and golden rain.
And in the distance, just like watercolor paintings –
Groves are squinting, and settlements muse…
   Ah, drink up, heart!
  The air is like a potion that's lost its strength.
  This is early autumn sending a kiss
  So wondrous yet sad.

I stand alone in unfamiliar fields,
Like an abandoned sacrifice.
And nature listens to my sorrow. Loving. Sincere.
   Through lament, through laughter.
  She herself – a kindly princess –
  Would bury her sorrow many times
  Within herself, in her songs.

I stand. I pray. So quiet-quiet everywhere,
As though before an icon of the Virgin.
Just from the villages, sorrowful bells soar in embrace.
   The patterns of tears.
  Only a crane's farewell to summer
  Comes sometimes from the clouds –
  Faded like the once dazzling silk of vestments…

Hey, by the road a willow stands
That catches ringing strings of rain
With all its branches swaying, sadly moaning:
   Sorrow, sorrow…
  I strum the strings of Sempiternity,
  This way for years, thus endlessly,
  I am a lonely willow.

           1915

O NATURE, DON'T CONCEAL...

O, nature, don't conceal, don't hide
That you're grieving for summer, you're mourning.
You're dreaming in mists... For some reason the owls
Have begun to weep in the meadow.

Because of sadness, because of sorrow
Your braids are covered with bloodstained gold.
Your heart surely must be gilded by sorrow,
For you are so tender, so.

But you once were like a storm with thunder!
Like the magic of St. John's Eve...[20]
Stillness and sorrow. Stillness and slumber.
Just a shooting star had fallen...

Oh, a star fell somewhere like a recollection.
My heart began to smile in longing.
Again the owls are sobbing... Oh, sob then, and pray:
Autumn is striding through the meadow.

1915

---

20   The Feast of John the Baptist in the Ukrainian Church calendar that occurs on June 24. The eve of the church holiday occurs near the summer solstice and is associated with ancient pagan rites. It is the time when nature is at fullest bloom, when fruits are ripening. It is the longest day of the year and the shortest night, therefore it is associated with magic. The folk belief exists that trees on that eve speak to one another and relocate themselves. He who finds the fiery fern blooming will become strong, will understand the language of animals and birds, will find great wealth – and will die. People gather healing and magical grasses on the day before. The sun is the central element to the holiday as a result of its association with the solstice. It is believed that at dawn the sun plays in all the colors of the rainbow and disappears and reappears in the water. For a literary realization of the folk belief see Nikolai Gogol's short story "St. John's Eve." The Eve is also associated with ancient fertility rites.

THE BIRDS ARE STILL...

The birds are still bathing the azure day in ringing songs,
The cloak of rye in golden waves is swaying in sunlight.
(The winds sprawl out, the winds are playing a harp);
And in the sky someone is already quarreling. A blue and black curtain
Covers half the sky in silence. The earth attires itself in shadow.
Man is hiding like an animal.
"God is coming!" Thought the wormwood.
The rain begins to cry... and tapers off.
The mountain grows silent. The valley grows still.
"God's shadow." The wormwood whispers.

And suddenly – the curtain tears in half! – Dead silence...
The fire scurries, blooms, and breaks up – even the waters seethe!
And a song flows out; a sacrifice is brought.
The dusty roads run off... And whirlwinds tear
The scant vein-like roots of old willows that pray in tears.
And the grass does not even dare to cry.
Mighty powers are coming! Darkness. Terror...
...And bells are ringing somewhere in a village.
Look – silver doves are already fluttering
Sowing calm in the sky.

1914-1916

IT'S DAWNING...

       It's dawning...
It's so quiet, so gentle, so soft in the field.
Distant poplars, like extinguished candles
In balls of incense, wrapped in the mists,
Play a melancholy scale in the soul.
       Little by little the day becomes...
It's so quiet, so gentle, so soft in the field.

       It's dawning...
Everything is still asleep: the sky as well as the faint stars,
Just a bird somewhere sleepily and lazily is spawning a sound,
And a burnt out stump, like a priest over a grave,[21]
Wails silently – "Have mercy, immortal one!"
With every second it's brighter.
Everything is still asleep: the sky as well as the faint stars,

       It's dawning...
The sunrise wounds the night with rays, with swords.
And golden clouds rush into battle.
Silent mists quiver above the fields.
And with them I stop for a morning prayer:
              Have mercy on us!
Why are You wounding our heart with swords?

1914-1916

---

21   One of Tychyna's variant versions of this line is "Ta temnyi bovvan na kozatskii mohyli" (And a dark stone idol on a Cossack grave)."

ENHARMONIES

FOG

Above the swamp milk is spun...
A black raven lost in thought.
A gray raven is musing.
It pecked out eyes. God knows whose.

And from the east wrath advances with swords!..
The black raven suddenly attacks.
The gray raven leaps up.
It pecked out eyes. God knows whose.

SUN

Somewhere the birds of paradise nibble
Green vines.
Lakes turned translucent!..

A shadow. Long ago.
The mowers mow before sunrise.
A flame of flowers!
A girl's breast sleepily says:
Son... my sweet son...

WIND

A bird – a river – a stalk of green vetch –
The rhythms of a sunflower.
The day runs, ringing-laughing,
It overtakes them!

Above the rye – it comes –
With goblets full of mead.
The day runs, ringing-laughing,
It overtakes them!

RAIN

On the water in someone's hand
Snakes writhe... A dream. To the bottom.

It blew, it puffed, it poured out grain –
And sparrows began to bound!..

"Run away!" something whispered to the shores.
"Lie down..." something shook the pines.
A tiny cloud dropped lace petticoats
Onto the meadows.

1918

THEY TRAMPLE FLOWERS...

They trample flowers, they trample the dew.
With honest,
Christ-resurrecting eyes
They weave poems.
But in their beauty you never sense
The sun.

      The kingdom.
The black-browed day has died.
To the singing of blood – without songs –
O knights of a mad knighthood.
Be damned to dung!

        – Rose-like!
        – Youthful!
        – Strife!

1917

TO THE CATHEDRAL

     I
Willows to one side.
Beggars to the other.
The willows bend and bend and bend.
The beggars stoop over.

The stirring of a deafened throng.
The flash of cloudy wings!
...The blue clattering of incensers
Swathes the pulpits.

Here they speak with God.
Here I'll tell Him –
(Someone began to cry outside the door) –
I'm serving with the cherubim!

I wait, the people anticipate –
But He isn't there.
The people bow and bow and bow.
Waiting for Him.

II
The path to the garden
Sings.
A pumpkin beneath leafy parasols
Contemplates the sun.

Beyond the picket fence
Is a green hymn.
Stay, good people, stay
With your nice little idols!

Sunflowers are ablaze...
 – just like a string –
Butterfly duets...
 – honey on its legs –

A daisy? "Greetings to you!"
She whispers back: "I greet you too."
The earth resonates
Like an organ.

1917

PASTELS

    I
A rabbit ran past.
Wow –
The dawn!
He's sitting and playing,
Opening the eyes of daisies.
The sky is fragrant at sunrise.
Roosters with fiery threads roll back
the black cape of night
 – the sun –
A rabbit ran past.

    II
The iron day
drank up some good wine.
Blossom, meadows! –
:I've been walking – for a day – [22]
Graze, herds! –
:to see my love – for a day –
Ears of grain like cradles sway! –
:during the day.
The iron day
drank up some good wine.

---

[22] Tychyna uses the colon at the beginning of lines to indicate quoted speech.

III

It was vibrating with flutes
Where the sun had set.
The evening approached
On tiptoe.
It switched on the stars,
It spread mists over the grass,
And, putting a finger on its lips,
Lay down.
It was vibrating with flutes
Where the sun had set.

IV

Cover me, cover me:
I'm night, I'm old,
I'm infirm.
My black road
Is eternally in dreams.
Place some mint here
And let the poplar rustle.
Cover me, cover me:
I'm night, I'm old,
I'm infirm.

1917

I WENT TO THE GROVE...

I went to the grove
to pick this flower – look!
and there the trees rock-a-bye
and the cuckoos always
coo
coo

I met a tiny rabbit
he was dozing on a hill
I would have caught him
but the cuckoo frightened him
coo
coo

1917

SOMEONE WAS CARESSING THE FIELDS...

Someone was caressing the fields, caressing them,
Walking about angry and sowing songs:
Oh, give us thunder, give us a downpour! –
May the golden manes not dry up.
Someone was caressing the fields, caressing them so gently...

Clouds floated like pearls...
Their pinkness – the lips of a child!
Shadows emerged – and... the valleys wait.
Shadows passed by and brought – sorrowful moments:
Clouds floated past, strange and distant...

Dazzling tones – and boundless freedom!
Oh, someone began to cry in the field.
An ominous fate, a cruel fate.
A slim poplar laughed in the distance.
Dazzling tones – and sad cornflowers...

1915

ON STEEP CLIFFS...

On steep cliffs
Where you find eagles and clouds,
Above the mighty sea,
In the radiant azure –
Hey,
Storms
Have blossomed there!
Storms have blossomed...

From the valleys
Hands stretched out to the skies:
O, thunderstorms, lend us
Your downpouring azure! –
At once
Downward
Droplets of blood fell!
Droplets of blood fell...

On tilled fields, on grass,
Silvery-green,
On slimstalked
Golden rye,
Hey,
There,
Where rustling rustled!
Where rustling rustled...

Someone burned daybreakingly,
Genuflectingly:
Earth, give us the rustling,23
The rustling – of madness!
The night.
Weeping.
Death rustles its scythe!
Death rustles its scythe...

August 1917

---

23   *Shum* is extraordinarily difficult to translate. Its primary meaning is "noise," but it can also mean rustle when used as an appellation for leaves, trees, the sea, etc. It also be translated as "peal," "din," "racket," "stirring."

A CHILD WENT OUT FOR BREAD...

A child went our for bread – rosily!
:run! they're shooting, they're coming.
He spread his tiny arms – rosily...

No God or devil – there will be a storm!
:hey, halt! we'll even get you in the churches.
The rooks took wing – there will be a storm...

August 1917

OPEN THE DOOR...

Open the door –
The bride is coming!
Open the door –
The azure blue!
Eyes, hearts, and chorales
                        Paused,
            Waiting...
The door was opened –
A dark, stormy night!
The door was opened –
All the roads in blood!
In unweepable tears
                        In darkness
          Rain...

1918

SORROWFUL MOTHER[24]

In memory of my mother

I

She passed through the field,
Through paths, through trails.
Pain illumined her heart
With lustrous knives.

She gazed – silence was everywhere.
A corpse was turning black in the rye…
Sleepily the spikes of grain refrained:
Rejoice, Mary!

Sleepily the spikes of grain refrained:
Remain, with us, remain!
The Blessed Mother halted and
Tears came.

There was no moon or stars,
But the day was slow in coming.
How frightful!…the human heart
Had grown so destitute.

II

She passed through a field –
The verdure grows green…
The disciples of her Son draw near:
Rejoice, Mary!

---

24 The imagery from this poem comes from the tradition of the *Khodzhennia*, the "walking" of the Blessed Virgin from the Apocrypha "The Virgin's Descent into Hell." In the story the Virgin descends into hell on Great Saturday. There she sees the tortured souls and pities them, allowing them to be released for one day. In the Eastern Slavic tradition, any land of sorrow becomes the land of Mary. For the Eastern Slavs, a native redeemer becomes a new Christ that grows out of the native land.

Rejoice, Mary:
We've been searching for Jesus.
Can you tell us the best way
To get to Emmaus?

Mary raised her hands,
As pale as lilies:
The road to Judea's not for you,
Turn from Galilee, too.

Go to Ukraine,
Stop in every home –
Perhaps there at least they'll show you
His crucified shadow.

III

She passed through a field.
A field rests covered with graves –
The wind blows in her face –
Christ is Risen,[25] Mary!

Christ is Risen? – I haven't heard.
I know not, I just don't know.
There will never be paradise
In this blood-spattered land.

Christ is Risen, Mary!
We are the flowers of St. John's Wort,[26]
We've sprouted in throngs from the blood
On the field of battle.

Distant villages remain silent.
The field is covered with graves –

---

25   The Ukrainian church hymn sung on Easter Sunday. The phrase is also used as a greeting at Easter time.

26   A literal translation of the word *zvirobii* here would be "beast slaughter."

And a flower implores, swan-like:
At least you be merciful, Mary!

IV

She passed through the field...
"Must such a land perish?"
Where He was born the second time,
A land that he loved till his death?

She looked – there was silence everywhere.
The wild rye is thriving.
For what have you been crucified?
For what have you been killed?

She couldn't bear the sadness
Or her torment
And fell to the trampled grass,
Her arms outstretched in a cross!..

Above her the spikes of grain
Whispered "Rejoice!"
But the angels in heaven above –
Neither heard nor knew.

1918

ALONG THE AZURE STEPPE...

Along the azure steppe
A raven-black wind!
It embraced me once and disappeared –
The raven-black wind...

I proceeded to reap the rye.
A thunderous storm cloud!
Not everyone comes back from war –
Raven-black wind...

The sun gazes like a child,
But in the villages there is famine!
Mothers walk, like shadows –
Raven-black wind...

In a foreign land somewhere far away
Without a cross; a raven...
Be damned together with war! –
Raven-black wind...

1917-1918

LULLABY

From Anatole Le Braz[27]

Go to sleep, little baby, go to sleep! May your dreams erupt in flowers!
Lord, protect those, whose path has led them to the seas!

Sing, old woman, pour your heart's pain into boundless, tender songs,
About the sea that glimmers in the moonlight: oh hush-a-bye...

When you get on the ship — then you can frolic!
The wind will make a cradle from the waves to rock you.

Sing, old woman, pour your heart's pain into boundless, tender songs,
About the sea that glimmers in the moonlight: oh hush-a-bye...

The song troubles your soul, the song endless, like the sea.
To the sons' delight, to their mother's grief.

Sing, old woman, pour your heart's pain into boundless, tender songs,
About the sea that glimmers in the moonlight: oh hush-a-bye...

A furious wave buried your father in the fiords!
You were being born just then, my son – but I did not sob.

Sing, old woman, pour your heart's pain into boundless, tender songs,
About the sea that glimmers in the moonlight: oh hush-a-bye...

The storm gathers monstrous clouds above the fiords.
It lulls black corpses to your rocking cradle.

Sing, old woman, pour your heart's pain into boundless, tender songs,
About the sea that glimmers in the moonlight: oh hush-a-bye...

---

27   Anatole Le Braz (1859-1926) was a popular Breton writer, ethnographer and educator, who collected and published a great amount of songs, stories and folklore to popularize the Celtic coastal region of France.

Go to sleep, little baby, go to sleep! May your dreams erupt in flowers!
Lord, protect those, whose path has led them to the seas!

Sing, old woman, pour your heart's pain into boundless, tender songs,
About the sea that glimmers in the moonlight: oh hush-a-bye...

But we give birth to you – o scorn! – and the depth will swallow you!
Whoever has been born a Breton – will have to die a sailor:

Sing, old woman, pour your heart's pain into boundless, tender songs,
About the sea that glimmers in the moonlight: oh hush-a-bye...

THE CHOIR OF BELL-FLOWERS

A fragment of a long poem

    Tiny Bells,
Bell-flowers,
           We praise the day.
    We sing,
We greet with ringing:
          The day-ding![28]
          The day-dong.

    We love the sun,
The sky and sun,
           The shadow bright,
    Dreams that delight,
Quiet meadows:
          Shady-ding!
          Shady-dong.

---

28   The rime riche couplet (*Den'/Den'* and *tin'/tin'*) at the end of each strophe imitates the sound of bells. Since this is impossible to duplicate in English translations, I have opted to add the onomatopoetic "ding/dong" to approximate the effect in the original.

    Float on, clouds,
Oh, bring on the torrents,
          A clear day.
    Sprinkle us,
Bless us,
          Day-ding!
          Day-dong.

    Let the shadow lie down along the field,
The golden field,
          The shadow will lie down.
    Let the rye sway –
The rye will smile:
          Shady-ding!
          Shady-dong.

1917

GREEN SUNDAY[29]

From its golden courtyard
Holy Sunday appeared.
It's quiet. Sad.
Nothing will fly by, or sing.
  – O Lord, send us a bird into the world!
It may be voiceless, but at least let it coo.
And God sent a cuckoo.
      – for your lifetime
      drink the music
      all the agony
      you, the accidental
      drowned one of our age –
Sad.
      Green Sunday.

1920

---

29   The "Green Holiday" occurs during the seventh Sunday after Easter in the Eastern Church and coincides with the celebration of the Descent of the Holy Spirit to the apostles on the fiftieth day after the Resurrection of Christ. The Spirit appeared to the apostles in the form of fiery tongues to inspire them with the task of spreading the Gospels to the people. In the Ukrainian tradition, churches and homes are adorned with greens. Graves of the departed are also adorned with green things to symbolize resurrection. The Ukrainian tradition has its source in ancient pagan rites and a belief in the sacredness of trees and their ability to keep away evil spirits.

WAR

    I
I lie down to bed.
Three angels stand in my head.
One angel – sees all.
The second – hears all.
The third – knows all.

And I dreamt
The Son.

That He alone is rising against the enemy,
And the enemy surrounds him and hacks at His breast!
(The first angel covers his face).

The field seems to be flat, flat and green.
And the wind sings: "Farewell, dear mother!"
(The second angel comes to me with a cross).

And the wind spreads out: "Do not grieve,
For whoever dies for Ukraine dies not!"
(The third angel cheers the heart).

And I dreamt
The son.

    II
To the right – the sun.
To the left – the moon.
And straight ahead – a star.

"I bless you, son, for battle with the enemy."
And he says: my mother dear!
It seems there never was
Or is an enemy.
We have only one enemy –
Our heart.

Bless me, mother, so that I may find an herb
To heal human madness.
I lifted my hand to bless him –
But suddenly no one was there.
Quietly, there was only a raven: cawing! cawing!

To the right – the sun.
To the left – the moon.
And straight ahead – a star.

1918

A *DUMA* ON THREE WINDS[30]

        In early spring, at the onset of spring,
        Hey, there was a clamor at sunrise.

Beyond the mountains tall,
Beyond the deep deep seas,
Beyond impassable paths –
Early in the morning the Bright Sun rose.
The Bright Sun rose, and summoned its brothers, the Winds,
    It proclaimed to them:
        "My brothers!
        My winds!
        My beloved dear brothers,
        So free and swift-winged!
        Stand up on your straight legs:
To mountains, to valleys, to human paths, to fallow fields
        Fly off – and sing,
        And tell the people
About me, your elder brother, the Bright Sun
 I'm not warming you like I did in winter:
Stars won't be able to wink at each other
    While I'm ablaze."

    The Winds heard all this,
    Stood up on their straight legs,
Spread their strong wings in many directions.

---

30   A *duma* is an epic oral verse form popularized by the kobzars, blind wandering minstrels, and *lirnyky*, players of the stringed folk instrument – the *lira*. The songs most often dealt with topics from the heroic Ukrainian past, particularly from the Cossack period. For a selection of the epics, see the volume *Ukrainian "Dumy"* (Cambridge: Harvard Ukrainian Research Institute, 1979) with an excellent introduction by Natalie Kononenko. This *duma* is an allegory with political implications. The first wind represents the Russian Provisional Government of Alexander Kerensky from the February-March Revolution of 1917; the second wind – the Bolshevik government that took power during the October-November Revolution of 1917; and the third wind – the Ukrainian Central Rada that took power in Ukraine from 1918-1919.

In early spring, at the onset of spring,
Hey, there was a clamor at sunrise.

The first young Wind –
Crafty Snowstorm –
Thought to himself and pondered:
"Wouldn't it be better,
If you, my brother, Bright Sun, rose in a wintry way?
For every time this earth warms up
Trouble follows."
So the first Wind – Snowstorm-Frost –
Flies, howls, and whistles,
Spatters houses with snow,
Laughs at people:
"Hi! It's the spring sun greeting you."

When the people heard this,
They proclaimed to one another:
"Spring looks about as likely as thunder on Christmas
When we're talked to in a strange tongue."

In early spring, at the onset of spring,
Hey, there was a clamor at sunrise.

The second young Wind –
Careless Stormy One –
Thought to himself and pondered:
"I don't care how the sun rises –
Whether wintry,
Or spring-like,
As long as I can carouse
To my heart's content."
So the second Wind flies upon the earth,
Knocks over peoples' houses,
And bitterly mocks:
"This is your spring and freedom," he says, "that greet you."

> When the people heard all this:
> They proclaimed to one another:
> "If this is spring, if this is freedom –
> > Then our fate is cursed!"

> > In early spring, at the onset of spring,
> > Hey, there was a clamor at sunrise.

The third young wind –
Caressing Gentle-Breeze-Warm-Winged-One –
> Thought to himself and pondered:
"Oh, thank God that the Sun has turned to spring,
Otherwise the earth would have chilled forever and died."
> Now the third Wind flies and sings,
> With tenderness, like a brother, he speaks to all in their native tongue,
> He misses not a single village, nor a single hut,
On a tattered pane with fingertips he taps and plays:
> "Arise," he says, "people, the Sun is smiling for you,
> > The earth awaits your plow."

Then all the people heard this,
Came out of their houses with songs,
And with great joy kissed the sacred earth –
> And gave glory to the Merciful Lord!

> > In early spring, at the onset of spring,
> > Hey, there was a clamor at sunrise.

1917

THE GOLDEN HUM[31]

Above Kyiv is a golden hum,
Both doves and the sun!
Below
The River Dnipro strums strings...

Ancestors.
Ancestors rose from their graves:
They walk through the city.
Ancestors bring sacrifices to the sun –
And that is why there is a golden hum.
O that hum!..
Because of it you can't hear your friend's words.
Because of it, storms sob as they fly through the city –
For no one pays them heed.

The golden hum!

At night,
As the Milky Way spreads its silvery dust,
Open your window and listen:
Listen:
Somewhere rivers flow in the sky,
The mighty rivers of pealing bells of the Monastery of the Caves and Sophia!..[32]
Golden vessels

---

31   "Homin" of the title is very difficult to find a single word in English that conveys its many nuances. I have opted for "hum" since it suggests the idea of voices talking. One might also translate it as "sound," "echo," or "chimes," which suggest the ringing of the bells of St. Sophia Cathedral and those of the Kyiv-Pechersk Monastery of the Caves.

32   The Kyiv-Pechersk Monastery of the Caves, where the relics of monks lie in crypts, is one of the most ancient monuments of Kyivan Rus civilization, lies above the banks of the River Dnipro. It was built under the reign of Prince Yaroslav the Wise in the mid-11th century. The Primary Chronicle was begun in the monastery at that time and provides the basic resource materials on the history of Kyivan civilization.

Of the far distant Past come to shore.
Golden vessels.
...Illuminated
Holding a cross,
Wounded by God's grace in his heart
Out steps the Andrew the First-Called.[33]
He mounts the hills:
Blessed be you, hills, and you, troubled river!
And the hills began to laugh,
Turning green...
And the troubled river filled with sun and azure –
And strummed the strings...

At night,
As the Milky Way spreads its silvery powder,
Come down to the Dnipro!
... God passes along the heavenly fields above the mustached
Old Man River,
God begins to sow.
Grains
Of crystal music
Fall.
From the depths of Eternity grains fall
Into the soul.
And there, in the temple of the soul,
Above which, in the unreachable heights, prayers swirl, like doves,
There,
In the sonorous temple the grains bloom into chords,
Inspired like the eyes of our ancestors.
It was, like a priest, drunken with prayer –
Our Kyiv –
Who prayed for all Ukraine –
Beautiful Kyiv.
                              – a storm!
Spontaneously he opened his eyes –

---

33   According to tradition passed down over the centuries, the Apostle Andrew in his journeys gazed upon what is now the Ukrainian land.

And laughter flows like wine...
                    – a flash!
                    – terror!
Unfurling bright banners
(And laughter flows like wine),
Kyiv suddenly arose in a blaze
In its creative flight!

:greetings! greetings! – are strewn from eyes.
Thousands of eyes...
Suddenly silence: someone speaks.
:hurrah! – is heard from a thousand chests.
And above all this doves in glow of the sun.
:hurrah! – is heard from a thousand chests.
Doves.
It was the Apostle Andrew,
Illuminated,
Wounded in the heart with God's grace,
Blessing Ukraine with a cross
For all the years of disgrace.
And the hills began to laugh,
Turning green.

But there are two black tombs,
And a bright one.
And all around
There are cripples.
They crawl, they whine,[34] stretching out their hands
(Oh, what misshapen fingers!) –
Give them something, give them something!
Give them something to eat – don't let them nourish the beast within,
 – give them something.
They crawl, they whine and curse the sun,
The sun and Christ!

---

34   Literally "whine nasally." In Ukrainian folklore, death speaks this way. I am grateful to Oksana Zabuzhko for pointing this out to me.

People pass:
the poor, the rich, the proud, the young, in love with clouds and music,
People pass.
A black bird – with talons for eyes! –
A black bird from the rotten corners of the soul,
From the field of battle it flew.
It caws.
O, soulless bird!
Is it not you who for ages
Pecked at the crucifixion of the human soul?
For ages.
Is it not you who gouged the eyes of the living,
And faith from the heart?
Faith from the heart.
What do you need now
In the hour of joy and laughter?
What do you need now, o, soulless bird?
                                      Speak!

Black wings over the doves and the sun –
Black wings.

"My brother, do you remember the spring days at the dawn of freedom?
Embracing, we walked along friendly paths,
We praised the sun!
And everyone (even the grass) laughed through their tears...
                                    "I don't remember. Go away."
"My dear, why don't you laugh, and why no joy?
It's me your brother, speaking to you in your native tongue,
Don't you recognize me?"
                       "Back off! I'll kill you!"

A black bird,
A black bird caws.
And the crippled
Are all around.
In hours of joy and laughter
Who put them on their knees?

Who told them to stretch out a hand,
Which mad deity – in times of joy and laughter?
The ancestors in terror turned away.

:we'll grow tall! said the poplars.
:we'll burst into songs! said the flowers.
:we'll overflow! said Old Man Dnipro.
The poplars, flowers, and Dnipro.

It rings, it rings, it rings
And breaks into pieces...
"Are these golden springs emerging from the earth?"
It sways, blows, caresses,
Trembles like a dream...
"Are these the gems that grow in the depths of hills?"

:we'll grow tall! they said.
:we'll overflow! said Dnipro.

In the starry morning lower your ear to the ground –
...they're coming.
From the villages and farms they're going to Kyiv –
By roads, by paths, by trampled tracks.
And their hearts beat to a common beat
 – they're coming! they're coming! –
They're ringing like suns to a common beat
 – they're coming! they're coming! –
There through the roads and paths and trampled tracks.
They're coming!
And laughter flows like wine:
And singing flows like wine:
I am a strong nation,
I am young!
I listened to your golden hum
And here I heard.
I looked into your eyes
And here I saw.
Heaps of rocks crashing down on my chest,

I took them off so easily
Like eider down...
I am the unquenchable Beautiful Fire,
The Spirit Eternal.
Greet us with the sun, with doves.
I am a mighty nation! – with the sun, with doves,
Greet us with native songs!
I am young!
Young!

THE PLOW
(1920)

Dedicated to my dear brother
Evhen Tychyna[35]

THE PLOW

Wind,
Not wind – a storm!
It smashes, it breaks, it upturns the earth.
Beyond black clouds
(With a flash! in blows!)
beyond black clouds a million million
                                      muscular arms...
It rolls. It cuts into the ground
(whether it's a city, a road, or a meadow)
A plow cuts into the earth.
And on the earth are people, beasts, and gardens,
and on the earth are gods and temples:
O, come, pass over us,
mete out your judgment!
And there were those who fled.
To caves, to lakes, and forests.
"What kind of power art thou?"
they asked.
And no one among them rejoiced or sang.
(The wind chased a fiery steed –
a fiery steed
in the night)
And only their dead, wide-open eyes
reflected all the beauty of a new day!
Their eyes.

1919

---

35   The poet's younger brother (1895-1955).

SOW SEEDS...

With a song, with play
sow seeds in the fertile black earth...
The sun stands tall as a mountain
Over the valley below!

Work – a beehive awakened.
The earth makes you sober:
from you, just from you I want just freedom –
and no venalities!

Be reckless – not cold.
It's time for the new Marcellaises!
Swing swords to the right and left –
put more sharps into the key![36]

Strike the brass, decloud[37] the sky!
Have faith (don't whine!), just go,
shout out fanfares into the night:
more sharps, more sharps into the key!

1919

---

36   A variant reading of "v kliuchi" could be: "in harmony."
37   A neologism created by Tychyna: *obezkhmarte*.

AND BELY AND BLOK...

And Bely and Blok, Esenin and Kliuev:[38]
Russia, Russia, Russia of mine![39]
...There stands Kyiv tormented a hundredfold,
and I, crucified two hundred times.

Yonder[40] everywhere is: the sun! – they're singing: Messiah! –
The mists, the valleys, a swampy road...[41]
Ukraine will raise its own Moses—
it has to be!

It can't be like this forever, I sense it, I know.
To laughter and storms, to the thunder of revolts,
from all my nerves into the steppe I send:
poet, arise!

---

38   Andrei Bely, pseudonym of Boris Bugaev; 1880-1934), the eminent Russian symbolist poet and novelist. He was an early supporter of the revolution. Alexander Blok (1880-1921), the great Russian symbolist poet who reacted to the revolution with his famous poems "The Twelve" and "The Scythians," and who later was apalled by its excesses and violence. Sergei Esenin (1895-1925), Russian imagist poet who found a great source of inspiration for his poetry in the Russian land. He committed suicide in 1925. Nikolai Kliuev (1887-1937), a Russian poet who glorified the Russian countryside and the peasant. He eventually died in a prison camp.

39   Tychyna uses extraordinary subtlety to make his point here: the word "Rossi_ia_" (Russia) in line 2 and "Mesi_ia_" (Messiah) in the vocative case as "Messi_ie_" in line 5 do not rhyme precisely. The slanting of the rhyme may very well indicate the incompatibility of Russia as the Messiah for Tychyna's Ukraine. The line echoes Andrei Bely's poem "Rodine" (To My Homeland). The pertinent lines from Bely's poem are: "Russia, Russia, Russia – /The Messiah of the coming day."

40   I.e., in Russia.

41   Reference to the city of Petersburg, Peter the Great's new capital of Russia, that was built in a swamp at the cost of thousands of lives, many of them Ukrainian serfs.

And the black earth rises up, staring me in the eye,
and distorts its face into bloody laughter.
Poet, to love your homeland isn't a crime
when you do it for the good of all!

1919

ON THE SQUARE...

On the square near the church
the revolution's marching on:
"Let the herdsman" – they all shouted –
"lead us as our chief."[42]

Say farewells, await your freedom,
to your horses, let's all go on!
With a bustle, with a murmur –
only the flags are blossoming tall...

On the square near the church
mothers have grown disheartened:
light up the road for them,
full moon, so high aloft!

Dust is settling on the square.
Voices are subsiding...
Evening.
Night.

1918

---

42   Literally *otaman* – the elected leader of a Cossack regiment or company.

HE FELL...

He fell from his horse
onto the white snow.
"Hurrah! Hurrah!" Rolled up to him
and lay at his feet.

How closely he pressed
his hand to his heart.
He would have been happy to see
another winter such as this.

They mowed down the enemy,
hey-ho, on all the fronts!
With a caw a raven sat on his chest,
a black raven-bird.

The revolutionary struck –
and all the world shook!
As he was dying in the open field –
he sent greetings to all.

1918

THEY OUTSTAR THE STARS...

They outstar the stars.
They outnight the night.
To the east lands every which way –
a sword! a sword! a sword!

With songs, with hammers! –
(the motif—a locomotive!) –
They come upon factories,
waters, fields of rye...

She has – puffed up breasts!
He's a locomotive! –
They come upon factories,
waters, fields of rye...

When they grow tired they'll embrace,
and go to the west lands again to sleep.
And from their fragrant bodies
dewy perspiration...

1919

IT WILL BE THIS WAY...

It will be this way –
blind men will ask: where is that sky – I can't see it?
Deaf men: it seems I would have heard the truth!
Cripples will moan: I'm crying,
I'm screaming from pain!

It will be this way.
Someone will pierce the false sky with laughter.
And the world will become new, and people will be like gods.
And everywhere that you'll find a field –
There will be plows, plows...

1919

INTERPLANETARY INTERVALS...

Interplanetary intervals!
The sun (everywhere this dream!), Jupiter...
And between them, not chorales –
But the wind

Mars – like a god! – Mars, Venus.
 – there everywhere you wait for a friend like the advent of God.
The eyes of a revolutionary,
Yearning

A shout in the interstellar womb:
We would bloom, we would drink the joyful wine! –
But the soul, the soul is captured
Alas

We would have been like grass, like greening crops...
But these same maledictions are everywhere!
Not octaves that cleave the heart –
But nonets[43]

1919

---

43   A musical composition requiring nine different musicians.

JUST BEYOND THE VILLAGE...

    Just beyond the village –
they shot them all,
stripping them,
mocking the dead
    in salute.

What a dreadful winter has come! –
You've got your freedom,
now you've got your contested fields,
with poplars at your heads,
    but there are no heads.[44]

When the night grew black –
something shone beyond the village,
walking about singing,
guarding, keeping vigil over
    the blameless massacre.

1918

---

44   *Holiv nemaie* could also be read as "there are no leaders."

AT SHEVCHENKO'S GRAVE...[45]

I
Having paid homage to the remains
we descended from the hill.
– Another tyrant, another captivity.
A steamship rasping far-off
smoked a cigar...
A dreamwave.
And suddenly across the Dnipro someone struck up a fire.
Someone leaned against pillars of rain,
Shuddering:
drink, earth, drink!
become drunk with rebellions!
...Stringed anger began to strum.
Trees and the landing began to move.
And the boats, like horses, grew frightened...
The red-blue-green rainbowingly said "hello"
                                        to all –
and it began to take in water.
And within me –
(stringed anger strummed) –
Oh, there'll still be a flood,
and laughter
and wine.

1918

---

45   The great Ukrainian bard's grave is located in the town of Kaniv on a tall hill overlooking the Dnipro River. Taras Shevchenko lived from 1814-1861. Freed from serfdom, he became the spokesperson for Ukrainian national consciousness for all succeeding generations. His slim volume of poems *The Kobzar* (1840) was a watershed in Ukrainian belles lettres and the primary impetus for a Ukrainian cultural revival in the 19th century. Shevchenko was exiled by the tsarist government for ten years in the 1840s. The gravesite in Kaniv is an obligatory shrine for all Ukrainians.

II
We stayed overnight on the floating Seagull Hotel.
Vasylchenko with his book *Karmeliuk*,[46]
and I – with my *Skovoroda*.[47]
I remember: on the river
the moon lost in meditation...
And on a veranda above the water
there were songs and cards at a table:
they came, just imagine, to Taras
from Pavlo Skoropadsky,[48]
from a swineherd!
They lamented: good doesn't exist,
but we want good for everyone.
It's time to "gather" our Russia!
We can serve Pavlo "by the by,"
and there...
The moon grew bloody along its edges.
The fellow from my village fell asleep.

...we won't let them out of our hands there!
Suddenly the water began to weep...
And there was no one to ask:
who should we expect to save Ukraine?
   – Karmeliuk.
   – Skovoroda.

1918

---

46   Stepan Vasylchenko (1879-1932), Ukrainian prose writer and dramatist and the author of the play *Karmeliuk* (1927), which was about the legendary leader of a peasant uprising opposed to serfdom. The leader of that uprising was Ustym Karmeliuk, who lived from 1787-1835.

47   *Skovoroda* is a book-length long poem that Tychyna began around this time. He never quite completed it, but spent the greater part of his life working on it.

48   (1873-1945). Skoropadsky was briefly appointed Hetman of the Ukrainian state during the German occupation of World War I. The so-called German-controlled "Hetmanate" lasted less than 8 months. Skoropadsky evacuated with the Germans on December 14, 1918.

III

Beyond Trypillia[49] on a mountain
Zeleny[50] was already thundering.
The turmoil had begun in Tarashchanka...[51]
 – rain, rain –
we went to Kaniv.
Cherry-tree streets, a bazaar.
The theater was like a cattle pen.
And below, toward the river, down from the Cathedral –
ravine after ravine...
Whom are they beating up? "This is freedom?"
 – "Shut up! can't the retaliation brigade
take a bribe?"
When will the vicious reptile die
and stop strangling the people!
We're going... "It's time!
It's time!" They're meeting us at the Seagull Hotel.
Time to go where? to escape? from whom?
We'll join the rebels, too – we laugh...

---

49   Trypillia, which literally means "three fields," is an ancient historic village near Kyiv.

50   Zeleny was the pseudonym of Danylo Terpylo, the leader of an army of Ukrainian nationalists that battled the Bolsheviks in the Trypillia region. The Bolsheviks defeated Zeleny's army in June 1919.

51   The Tarashchanka district in the summer of 1918 was the site where a Ukrainian partisan army of 30,000-40,000 peasants was organized to battle the occupying German troops, inflicting heavy casualties on them.

And someone said:
wait,
Vynnychenko[52] lives here somewhere.
...O Prince Mountain![53]
is so very high.

1918

---

52   Volodmyr Vynnychenko (1880-1951). Ukrainian prose writer and dramatist who became the leader of the Central Rada of the independent Ukrainian republic in 1918. After the Bolsheviks overthrew the newly formed government, Vynnychenko emigrated to Paris where he continued to write.

53   Located in Podillia, one of the oldest sections of the city of Kyiv, it is the site of the Cathedral of St. Andrew. It is traditionally the area where all the princes of Kyiv lived.

THE MESSIAH

I imagine –
(a terrifying moment!) –
He will come, burst into tears from despair
and darken the sun.
Someone will toss in a drunken word:
"Execute them! down to the pavement!"
And the moon will rise
anticipating a fire.
Instead of rain, instead of dew –
Stones from the sky...
And someone's voices:
"Don't! Don't!"
A cripple, rushing somewhere, will step on a child.
And everyone will shout without end:
"Messiah! Greet the Messiah!"
"Hosanna to Him, He has come!"
And blood
will remake mortal ecstasy into a cherished dream.

1918

FROM THE CYCLE "CREATION OF THE WORLD"

          I
In the beginning there was nothing –
    other than might
        and movement!

In the beginning instead of God
    there were fiery wings,
        and a spirit over everything…

And fire raised its palms:
    blithe tempests! –
        or so the fog thinks.

Red choirs grew silent.
    And cliffs rose.
        The ocean began to roar…
the first day

          II
The gray evening has already nodded off.
    Eve has fallen asleep – quietly.
    The flock is reposing – night.

Adam emerged from his tent.
    He comes and stands before – a cave.
    He starts up a fire – and forges.

Stars did shine.
    Eve woke up – quietly.
    "Is the iron ringing?" – night.

She came: "go to sleep!" – he doesn't hear.
    Adam stands – lost in thought.
    And beside him – a plow.

the second day

III
They let the poor be sacrificed
to the land and capital.
      Like tsars they sit on a throne themselves.

"We're here below, the gods – above.
Go to the factories and quarries,
    you, damn beggars!"

The poor shouted out: near and far!
Not telegrams of congratulations,
     but a bullet in the brow for the profiteers!

Let's slice them with our sharpest blades!
         For all the lands –
   a Marcellaise!

the day before the last

1918

LETTERS TO A POET

A Triptych

       I

A map of Hellas, a book by Kotsiubynsky,[54]
on a bookshelf a swan:
this here is all my room –
stop by just any time!

I welcome you like a friend.
Ah, I've waited for you for a while,
ever since I've laughed and cried
over your book of poems.

I always dream of: the sun, songs,
of You, of a spring day –
and now finally I've met You,
my dearest poet.

Come over today: I'll be home all alone
just me and my flowers.
I'll wait for you all evening,
in trepidation but with joy...

      II

You seem, maybe, not to be from these parts,
or... o, no, I don't dare.
I read You – but I don't quite
understand it all.

Whether I'm in a field or in the forest –
it always seems to me:

---

54   Mykhailo Kotsiubynsky (1864-1913). Outstanding Ukrainian prose writer best known for his short stories as well as the novella *Shadows of Forgotten Ancestors* (made into an award winning film of the same title by Sergo Paradjanov) and the novel *Fata Morgana*.

the stuff in your book isn't alive
while here it's all alive and happy...

Someone wrote recently that you're:
"The jewel of our poetry."
All the same You're not quite the same
as our bard Taras.[55]

You write about it all: about our people,
about the country's plight.
But I can't take it all to heart –
Try and I might.

III

I'm a communist girl, wearing foreign clothes,
I've cut off my braid.
Isn't it shameful for You to sing
now about the sun, about beauty?

I'm writing to You because I had the urge.
Tell me:
who needs these rickety
sonnets and songs?

The people, you'll say? the hungry?
The hand that feeds the worker
with triolets is really pathetic
and disgraceful.

Bye for now, but don't be surprised –
that this isn't a love letter.
But I'll say anyway: You're quite a force,
and someday You'll make a communist.

1920

---

55   See note #36 for a discussion of Ukrainian bard Taras Shevchenko.

MADONNA OF MINE...

    I
Madonna of Mine, Immaculate Virgin,
exalted in eternity!
Only the wind is blowing
on our lonely altars...

Pass over us wearing an omophorion,[56]
sob above the village.
We'll no longer sing songs or psalms to you
with our strange choir.

 – A dauntless woman, a sinful virgin
proceeds toward us.
Naked – unclothed, unadorned –
she charms us like a blooming rose.

Lean over, Madonna, against the side
of the last house in the village.
Smile – and then leave through the plowed fields,
flicking away bullets like bees...

    II
Already they sing and exalt
    a new name.
(Ave Maria,
My guelder rose!)[57]

She walks and laughs:
    life! a flower!
The sun into a fiddle,
and clouds begin a dance.

---

56   See note #18.

57   The guelder rose (also called a snowball tree) is the traditional symbol of Ukraine. The bush has red berries like the cranberry, and when it blooms, puffy white flowers.

A hand rests
      on hips, as though on strings.
Hello, girl,
who do you belong to?

I'll say – I won't:
      I'm everyone's, I'm yours...
(Ave Maria,
My guelder rose!)

      III
My Madonna, Blessed Virgin,
my Bluest Flower!
A pure soul
steps into a new era.

Lips kiss a rose
instead of a lily.
Yet I can not deny You
as Peter did to Christ.

With whom now, at what hour
will I be rejuvenated again?
Can it be I won't pray even once
for my love, for humankind?

Iron resonated. Concrete is silent.
Year after year.
Strum in my heart, My Golden Dream,
in various tones...

IV
Not of stone, not of marble –
but made of simple iron.
    – Tender, bold,
    oh where is your chiton?

Where is your golden cassock,
your sorrowful eyes? –
    A strummed hosanna,
    a cornflower tone.

Till night we'll toil
in the field as though in a cathedral.
    Ripen – fill out
    with the rye-fields in unison!

With songs, with embraces
our madonnas will meet us.
    A late... iron... dream
    above their breasts...

1920

A PSALM TO IRON

    I
We hate accursed copper,
concrete and raw iron!
Oh, what's that in the field, what's that sound –
is it Tartars, Turks, or Huns?

We emerge in the morning as though from a cave –
it's smoldering throughout the land!..
Swords instead of flowers, spears
glisten in the valley...

It bursts – it strikes – it thunders through,
growing quiet beyond the mountain –
already it's rushing, already it's roaring
high over our heads;

it kicks with its hoof, begins to roar,
tosses a gray storm cloud –
and with a shout into the sky
a new psalm to iron rises.

    II
Somewhere beyond the seas there is law and honor.
Beyond the ocean there is conscience.
If only the train station would run, would roar,
would rouse industry!

The city is sick: a cough, blood.
Crows and jackdaws at the corpse...
Only sometimes, as if in a dream,
music and catalfalques can appear.

And a rumor circulates: the general
escaped from the city in the morning.
They'll probably surrender without a battle
when the rebels surround them.

A factory is quiet – it doesn't drink or eat,
mold has filtered in from below...
And silently into the sky
a new psalm to iron rises.

    III
The blessed hour passed like a dream
of the Gothic and Baroque.
An iron renaissance approaches,
and squints its indifferent eye.

It's all the same to us, God, or the devil –
both of them are generals for us! –
Cathedrals raised their eyebrows,
the city's neighborhoods scattered.

Above the city are wails and laments,
like feathers from a feather bed...
The early green evening
fainted, shouted, and fled.

What's burning here: an archive, a museum?
throw on some kindling!
with a curse into the heavens
a new psalm to iron rises.

    IV
What the hell do we need power for?
Give us some bread, something to eat! –
And communists march and sing
behind the insurrectionists.

Wait comrades,
we'll be eating and drinking yet.
Just help us
smash the capitalists.

The workers walk on
in a cheerful gait.
Covered in ribbons and flowers,
just like a young bride.

The sun coos in the trees,
a turtledove along a cornice...
Into the sky in red
a new psalm to iron rises.
1920

RONDELS

I

I walk from work, from the factory
to meet a demonstration.
Decked in flowers, all the streets shout:
long live freedom, long live freedom!
The sun laughs from the sky,
the clouds rush by somewhere on horses…
I walk from work, from the factory
to meet a demonstration.

What a beautiful spring! What beautiful nature!
In my heart sunbeams resound…
"To wed the rabble with the land!
Only then will there be eternal harmony."
I walk from work, from the factory.

II

The poplars mobilize
beneath the cloudy wind on a hill…
We have been ready for a long time,
we've been calling all for a long time: to freedom!

To freedom, the poor, the barefoot, and naked!
it's not time to sit in a burrow!
The poplars mobilize
beneath the cloudy wind on a hill…

We'll shout to the world about our pain!
So that from our planet to the stars –
all the proletarians everywhere would hearken
to what we fight for, here, in the field!
The poplars mobilize…

1920

FEBRUARY 26 (MARCH 11)[58]

I
There on a mountain beyond the Dnipro
banners are happily shouting:
honor to him, glory, and praise!

Orchestras play, and the churches
hail his portrait in flowers –
there, on a hill, beyond the Dnipro

The singing rolls into the steppes,
moving from village to village:
honor to him, glory, and praise!

Let's rise, little brothers,
let's welcome our prophet.
There on a hill beyond the Dnipro
honor to him, glory, and praise!

1920

---

58   The great Ukrainian bard Taras Shevchenko's birthday.

II

The preacher men and dictators came (oh shame!), –
just the ones You could not abide.
And someone erected Your bust
between the monastery and the cathedral.

You stand. You stare into the distance with reproach...
What fire was burning in your soul
when you awakened and summoned the blind bards,[59]
to fight the violence, kingdoms and terror!

Well, what of it, Taras! If you're happy about it or not –
look how things are here these days,
in one great family, in a society free.[60]

Look. Keep silent. Even if you get hungry –
say nothing to the First-Enthroned-One. – [61]
Otherwise they'll even label You a chauvinist.

1920

---

59 A "Kobzar" is a blind bard who wandered from town to town playing the *kobza*, a lute-like instrument. The kobzars sang epics and *dumy* of the heroic Ukrainian Cossack past. They were usually led around by a sighted orphan boy and lived off of the good graces of people who would feed and house them. *Kobzar* was the title of Shevchenko's first pathbreaking collection of poetry that was published in 1840. The title *Kobzar* has since become synonymous with Shevchenko himself.

60 A close paraphrase of lines from Shevchenko's poem "Zapovit" (My Testament; 1845), in which the poet asks to be buried on a hill overlooking the River Dnipro and the steppes.

61 I.e., Moscow.

I KNOW…

I know: the new bards, the new beauty, the rabble
will damn you more than once –
since you didn't find the road to freedom
from that native swamp of yours.

They'll question you, they'll drag you to trial:
you glorified sloth, but what of toil?
Why, instead of a boat, did you set out a raft,
Terrified of what is called Essence?

Enough of sleep! step out onto the road!
A hymn to Man, to Humanity, and not to God!
The glorious gift – of the entire soul to the future!

Burn! Look straight into the eyes of the sun!
For the world moans from "genius"-hacks,
And even you won't get to live twice…

1919

FOR HNAT MYKHAILYCHENKO[62]

We can't imagine you decaying,
or lying in the damp earth –
because you'll always live on and burn,
because your spirit will blaze on forever.

You'll yet be resurrected and dawn,
you'll arise in millions and seethe:
why, people, why are you asleep,
why aren't you courageous, why don't you dare? –

Tyrants have tortured you to death...
Marcellaised worlds
have set out to mourn and grieve.

We take an oath: in the hour of victory –
to fight to the death – but we'll vanquish the enemy!
O brother of ours, o beloved, brother of ours...

1919-1920

---

62   Ukrainian proletarian writer who, along with Vasyl Blakytnyi, helped form the literary group "Borot'ba" (The Struggle) in 1918. He was executed in 1919 by Russian White Army forces under the command of General Anton Deniken.

ONE ESCAPED IN LOVE…

One escaped in love, another in mysticism,
a third to the mountains where eagles fly…
And then they gave away the Ukrainian muse
to some schoolboy.

And now they churn out copies
of saccharine Russian women poets.
They go from utopia to utopia –
and call it "Sagesse."[63]

But the genuine muse is demusified
at the front somewhere, in the dry night
she lies spit upon and husked
on the Ukrainian highway.

Why do we scream then, the blind, the deceived:
"Only those with makeup on are poets"
why do we smoke cigarette butts
and tighten ourselves in a corset?

Has our nation grown weary,
or is it close to the end –
because we have splendid profanation
yet almost not a single bard?

And almost no poem
that would move us! – None.
Only the harbingers of anesthesia
and bewilderment alone…

1919

---

63   "Wisdom" or "sagacity" in French.

FOR SHRIVELLED PROPHETS

To you, poets of the state, petty waiters,
to you I give my word, my wrath.
Don't make romanticism
from the red blood of your brothers!

Become drunken with glory, with wine,
call yourselves the high priests of beauty –
but don't cry, don't wail over coffins
like dogs.

You find false aestheticism and grace
even at gravesites.
What can a universal federation mean for you,
corrupt merchandisers of inspiration and slaves?

What can brotherhood mean when you have eroticism? –
Shut up, move away from the graves!
From you, as though from a crooked wick,
the Revolution just smolders...

1920

BURN THE PROCLAMATIONS...

Burn the proclamations, trample the decrees:
accursed bayonets are goring us again!
Curse the laws and bureaucratic rabies –
Freedom! – let it be the only order.

Freedom! freedom! – the heart is pounding...
Again they're crucifying us like slaves before the people.
Again there are shackles, prisons, and ramrods,
and the captive word is hidden beneath coattails.

Who has the right to coerce a man?
Who can turn night into day?
And who's so wise to hang us all together
for the truth, our only sin?

Burn the proclamations, trample the decrees:
accursed bayonets are goring us again.
Curse the laws and bureaucracy's rabies –
Freedom! – let it be the only order.

1919

INSTEAD OF SONNETS AND OCTAVES
(1920)

INSTEAD OF SONNETS AND OCTAVES

Dedicated to Hryhory Savych Skovoroda[64]

It's dawning, but still there's mist...
A frown has fallen over the sky.
"*What* sadness has come to me!"

Radiant furrows have plowed into clouds.
I hear fanfares!
"*What* sadness has come to me!"

Oh, those aren't fanfares, but *surmas*[65] and cannons.
Lie still, mother, don't awaken!

Damnation to all, damnation to all, who've become beasts!
(Instead of sonnets and octaves).

AUTUMN
Over all cultures of the world May mold has grown.

Autumn. In the cities by four o'clock street lamps already are lit.
And in the village when the shepherd's shadow reaches ten paces
The flocks are still driven home.

---

64   Skovoroda (1722-1794) was a Christian philosopher, who late in his life became a holy wanderer. Often called the Ukrainian Socrates, he propounded belief in the duality of man. He divided the world of man into the visible and the invisible, the corporeal and the divine. His philosophy centered on man, with a belief that every individual's task was to bring his two natures into harmony in order to achieve peace. The Bible for Skovoroda offered the symbolic means of synthesis for man's two natures. In part Skovoroda provided the source for the title of Tychyna's first collection of verse, *Clarinets of the Sun*. Skovoroda considered the sun to be the macrocosmic center of the visible world, and in a sense worshipped it symbolically. In *Instead of Sonnets and Octaves*, Tychyna dialectically counterposes that sunny, illuminating moral and spiritual tradition of Skovoroda with the horrors of war and revolution, a return to the pre-Christian era of violence and the law of the beast.

65   *Surmas* are native Ukrainian instruments in the horn family.

They said: you can buy some old regal crimson fabric,
somehow cover a rubbish heap and enthrone culture (you
just have to hold up its head!) – perhaps, again it
will speak to us.

And leaves fell. But the head did not hold up on the neck.
Then – they threw themselves into eclecticism. They took a little brick
and the same amount of music. They thought – it'll work out well...
And leaves fell. But the head failed to hold up on the neck.

Over all the cultures of the world May mold has grown.

ANTISTROPHE[66]
Grown-ups and seven-year-olds sing:
    "O, sweet apple, where are you rolling?"[67]
Yes. The nation's at pasture and the poets in furrows.

Enough of looking grimly at the workshop: the Forerunner's always
less talented than the Messiah.

TERROR
Once again we take the Gospels, philosophers, poets. The one
who said "it's a sin to kill" the next morning lies with a bullet
in his head. And dogs fight over the body on a garbage heap.

Lie still, mother, don't awaken!

The great idea demands sacrifices. But is it a sacrifice
when a beast eats a beast?

---

[66] A paired strophe in ancient lyric poetry and tragedy, often used to examine the same idea from opposite points of view. The anti-strophe is also the second component of the Pindaric ode. The chorus sang the strophe while moving in one direction, the anti-strophe while moving in another, and the epode while standing still. So the structural division of the poem reinforces Tychyna's philosophical conflict, which becomes resolved in the poem's final line.

[67] The line comes from the Russian *chastushka* "Iablochko" (The Little Apple), which was a popular cycle of songs sung during the Revolution.

– don't awaken, mother...

Cruel aestheticism! – but when will you stop
admiring a slashed throat?

A beast eats a beast.

ANTISTROPHE
Airplanes and the perfection of technology – what good is it
when people don't look each other straight in
the eye?

Don't take the wicked to prison: they are
their own prison.

Universities, museums, and libraries will not give
what
brown,
gray,
and blue eyes can...

ROCK-A[68]
I sleep – can't sleep. I bow to someone else's will. I rock-a-.
And somehow suddenly there is abundance! Rock-a-bye...

Cockerels (a window) and the flood tide of green beer (through
the window) – the sound of "O" is everywhere.[69]

---

68   The Ukrainian original reads "Liu," which is the typical first person singular ending of Ukrainian verbs and also the reduplicated component of the verbal form in Ukrainian meaning "I love" (*liubliu*). "Liu" is also part of the word "liuli," which is typically used in Ukrainian lullabies. Tychyna plays on the sound throughout this strophe in the original text.

69   Wasyl Barka has explained this image as Tychyna's effort to build a sonatina in several keys – one of them "o" [Unpublished letter to Michael Naydan, May 22, 1980]. In this strophe the original text contains a number of assonances and alliterations of the sound "l," "o," and "iu."

"I don't understand." Marcel Etienne! Marcel Etienne!"⁷⁰
they shouted holding banners. Now they're rotting in the ground.
You say that even I will die?

Through all of life a legato has spread (a factory whistle).
Enough of that! Turn my fate blue, too. Rock-a-bye...
But it's just a bird outside the window singing: triplets, triplets!

And what about beauty? And immortality? – I remember
(it's even funny): "for an eternity with you!" my love swore an oath.
Evidently only in spirit are people enharmonious. For all
tragedies and dramas are consonances in the end.

"Arise!" "A new power has entered the town!"
I open my eyes ("consonances").

On the wall from the sunbeams, the lattice-framed window
forms a fiery sharp...

ANTISTROPHE

Even when above boundless water
herds of winds grazed;
Even when mountains quivered, the earth cracked,
and along the rough grass, sharp as swords, various monsters
crawled –

– Clouds, carefree clouds played in the sun.
Tender childlike forms! – delicate outlines! – who
needed them?

A savage, having eaten his fill of raw meat, followed them
for a while with blank eyes while vacantly sniffing
a flower
that looked like thistle.

---

70   Etienne (d. 1358) led a revolt of citizens in Paris in 1357-1358 opposed to the French king Jean II.

THE HIGHEST POWER
"Get dressed for a firing squad!" someone shouted
and knocked at the door.

I awoke. The wind opened the window. The sky was turning
green and clearing. And above the entire city
an immense grand piano played...

And I understood. Easter had come.

ANTISTROPHE
I'll never love a woman without
a musical ear.

I pray not to the Spirit himself nor to Matter.

By the way: without music socialism can't be established
by any cannons.

RHYTHM
When two slender girls walk – with red poppies
in their hair –
– you think of somewhere far away! of young planets!

They float. They glide. Atoms of fatigue to the world,
into the light from darkness. They dance, raise dust... Suns
stand in a ring. And from them there's a fluttering
through the whole universe.

Two girls.

ANTISTROPHE
She poured some milk for the hungry children and sat down
lost in thought...

As though from blind eyes tears were rolling down a jug.
The first quicker, down. The second,
followed after

as if
reluctantly...

Two girls.

EVOHE[71]

The creators of the revolution are, for the most part, lyric poets.
The revolution is a tragic lyric, and not a drama
as it's rumored.
Evohe!

Our offspring will train to walk behind a plow
no less than they now practice in a ballet studio. And
anyone who won't know the song will be treated
like a true counterrevolutionary.

Everything in the world depends on squinting eyes.
Evohe!

ANTISTROPHE

Join the party, where they look at a human being
as a world treasure, and where they all are one against
the penalty of death.

Let them call you creators behind closed blinds,
sentimentalists... Is it so important?

In our country to this day they don't throw ashes on the garden,
but somewhere in a corner beneath a fence.

WHO'LL SAY

The rain dripped a little – and all the sidewalks now have
typhus...

---

71   A shout of exclamation at ancient Greek festivals often associated with Bacchanalian revelers.

The young novelist says: "I don't want to, I can't write!
The city weighs you down, life gets on your nerves."

I was silent. Somewhere nearby a bomb...

"If we could only, say, go to the village. Bathe, walk
through the dew."

"Kill the saboteur!" I read on
one of the posters.

And behind us were beggar women,
extending their hands –

ANTISTROPHE
Grass grows wherever it wants. The wind tosses an order for
mobilization into a puddle. "Some milk!" a child cries,
but there isn't even a scrap of bread.

Who'll say: that there is a counterrevolution?

CHAUVINISTICALLY
They take bread, coal, sugar, and repeat as though in
a toast:
"Well, may God grant you fortune...may we often continue
to eat dumplings in your land.
And, suing a neighbor about the fence, we respond:
"So be it, so be it..."

Sometimes it's like this: the sky is clear,
                         but water's drippings from the eaves.

ANTISTROPHE
The rightists go back, but they try to hold their head
forward.

The leftists rush forward, but they've turned their heads back.

No matter how much you praise the teachings of Christ,
he still rode on asses and welcomed hosannas.

A TEST
As soon as we began to love the land, took
a spade in our hands and rolled up our pantlegs...
"For God's sake, pull up your cuffs, tell them
something: they're asking if we have culture!"

Some lanky foreigners smoked through a *pince nez*.

And misery is all around – like tall weeds, like sugar-beet leaves!
And everywhere the earth is trampled, bright red...

Skovoroda once walked here.

ANTISTROPHE
The most profound, the loftiest and, at the same time,
the simplest content is composed of two or three
notes – that's a true hymn.

Not for contests, and not for awards, write
a contemporary "Christ is Risen."[72]

EMPTINESS
I wash. The water's like metallophones. A curtain –
the wind with banners!

In the courtyard are poplars and women.
"But I'll tell you: the town is completely surrounded."
"Oh, my world!.."

The window was shut. Water quivers in a pitcher – a fan
whirling on the ceiling...

---

72   A Ukrainian church hymn sung on Easter Sunday.

– It was yesterday that the workers at the factories...
(– – – clearly you can hear the cannonade).

It looks like rain.

ANTISTROPHE
The city is decked out in painted posters: a person
stabbing another.

We read the list of the executed and are surprised
by pogroms in the provinces.

Everything can be justified by a lofty purpose – but
not the emptiness of the soul.

TARES[73]
They shoot the heart, they shoot the soul – they
pity nothing.[74]

...A child sat at the window, stuffing her fingers into her mouth,
peering out for her momma. But mother is lying in the street
with a half pound of bread in her hand...

Over the twentieth century
linger tares and Parsifal.[75]

---

73   Alternate translations for this word include: darnel, furrow-weed, pasque-flower, or flower bell. An intoxicant, the weed symbolizes evil. It occurs in a parable from Matthew XIII: 24-30, in which an enemy sows tares among a good man's wheat. Rather than dig up the tares immediately, the good man orders his servants to allow them to grow until the wheat is ripe. At harvest time they will first uproot the tares and burn them, then harvest the wheat and store it in the barn. Christ uses this parable to explain judgment day. Those who have led righteous lives will be harvested in heaven, while the evil, like the tares, will be burned in hell.

74   A close paraphrase of line 4 part 11 of Aleksandr Blok's famous long poem about the Revolution of 1917, *The Twelve*.

75   The hero Parsifal occurs in *Parsival*, an opera in three acts by Richard Wagner (completed in 1882) that was based on the Wolfram von Eschenbach

ANTISTROPHE
It's still not a revolution just to play Scriabin
for the prison guards.

The Eagle, a Trident, a Hammer and Sickle[76]...and each
acts as your own.

But a rifle has killed our own.
Our own gun lies at the bottom of our soul.

Should I, too, kiss the slipper of the Pope?[77]

---

medieval German romance *Parzival* written in the early thirteenth century. Perhaps most significantly for Tychyna, Parsival in his quest for the Holy Grail suffers from estrangement from God but struggles on behalf of the good.

76   The eagle is the emblem of tsarist Russia, the trident the emblem of the short-lived free Ukrainian republic, and the hammer and sickle the symbols of the new communist state after the revolution in 1917.

77   Yuri Lavrynenko interprets this line to refer not to the Roman pope, but rather to the Russian "pope" (i.e., Lenin) [See his article "Na shliakhakh syntezy kliarnetyzmu," *Suchasnist'*, 7-8 (1977), 91.]. The association of the papacy with Lenin and Russia has its historical basis in the messianic concept of Moscow as the third Rome, propounded first by the Russian abbot Filofei of the Pskov Monastery in a letter to Basil III in 1510. After the fall of Constantinople to the Turks in 1453, Ivan the Great married the niece of the last Byzantine emperor in 1472, thereby creating an historical link between Moscow and the Byzantine Empire. Filofei in his letter to Basil writes: "The Church of ancient Rome fell because of the Apollinarion heresy; as for the second Rome – the Church of Constantinople – it has been hewn by the axes of the Ishmaelites, but this Third new Rome – the Holy Apostolic Church, under thy mighty rule, shines throughout the entire world more brightly than the sun.... Two Romes have fallen, but the Third stands, and no fourth can ever be...." Filofei's letter makes that distinct connection with Skovoroda's sun imagery, showing that even in the late fifteenth and early sixteenth centuries, Russia's messianic goal was to outshine the sun. Tychyna ultimately presents two kinds of sunlight in his poem: Skovoroda's sunlight of peace and love, and the Soviet sunlight, which threatens to outshine Skovoroda's.

IN THE ORCHESTRA OF THE COSMOS
(1921)

IN THE ORCHESTRA OF THE COSMOS

    I
Blessed be:
Matter and space, number and measure!
Blessed be the colors, and timbres and fire,
the fire, the tonality of the whole world,
    fire and movement, fire and movement!

O, Spirit, that has imbued all,
    who art thou?
Should you be called tranquility? or the wind?
the blind power of the machine?
Or the musical ear of atoms, the play of specks of dust?

Before the whole world you raised your hands, as though before
a music stand,
the background
began to hum like propellers,
chaos began to whirl in a dance,
and somewhere trombones reverberated in bottomless corridors...

Countless multitudes of bodies, of unwelded bits quivered in solitude:
    faster, faster
    one with the other
    orbitally in a flow we will fall,
    faster!

    Millions of solar systems
    vibrate, tear, and roar!
    Comets neigh and race,
    and oceans resound over oceans.

    Countless multitudes of bodies, of unwelded bits,
    spiral downward, to the side, up to the ceiling...
        Flames! flames!

And rays of light cry and sing into the distance
like violoncellos.

Spirit that has imbued all,
who art thou?

  II
I am spirit, the spirit of eternity, of matter. I am primordial muscles.
I am the spirit of time, the spirit of measure and space,
            the spirit of number,
Aerolite rivers begin to flow
From a single splash of my oar...

I am a striving spirit, I am a tank-rhythm, choruses of cars,
my garage-yard vibrates with engines.
And I, with such ease, lead titans to space
just like children to the beach.

Layer upon layer I arrange solar systems
On water.
I compose youthful thoughts,
I give them musical themes.

  And off they fly,
  through streams they flow.
  Until they sink –
  I will not leave or go.

  Fly, fly, steer toward the suns,
  steer onto the globular sky dome.
  Summon everyone and federate all,
  Spread the slogans among the worlds.

  Attach no meaning to Saturn's crowns:
  Stop living for yourself, so callously!
  For all the planets, all the suns
  freedom, equality, and brotherhood!

And off they fly,
through streams they flow.
Until they drown –
I will not leave or go.

I am spirit, the spirit of eternity, of matter, I am primordial muscles.
I am the spirit of time, the spirit of measure and space,
                                    the spirit of number,
Aerolite rivers begin to flow
From a single splash of my oar...

III

In the orchestra of the cosmos
all must obey a single hand.
There are no boundaries... and where are those limits,
that would mark the semesters of the sun
in the azure milk?

Ether floats, the wind strums,
springs beat out new poems,
constellations rise up in the form of letters
with a radiant fire all around.

And what use is time there? And what use a century[78]?
And what of the concepts "day" and "morning?"
A crimson shout, a bloody shout,
protuberances of red suns!

No sadness there, no sorrow or oppression,
the systems have no egotism.
There each knows his own orbit,
the law, the law of socialism.

There each one knows those like himself:
Companion – friend – comrade – brother.

---

78   Or: lifetime.

And every world-aerostat
comes to meet at every instant.

One will fall – another will throw off sparks,
without bounds and without end...
And neither planets nor suns
have any right to stop.

In the orchestra of the cosmos
all must obey a single hand.
There are no boundaries... and where are the limits
that would mark the semesters of the sun
in the azure milk?

    IV
What are our tears, our screams and shouts?
What are all the dramas of the earth in the tragedy of the Cosmos?

Eternally young, primordial and wild,
a creator, crucified on his own creation –
it is he who raves in depthless depth and seethes without bounds!

His lungs exhale storms!
His heart would embrace the tiniest atom!
And his brain rends thought like dynamite!
Mad vessel, breasted with sails,
an anchor that cannot moor above abysses in song –
like Prometheus he sobs to the future
and never returns.
Tears break forth,
waters of the ocean break out and smash against eternity.
Sprays bounce away and are scattered!
Sprays like sparks from flint!
Sprays to far off worlds!
Tell us: what are the solar systems if not sprays?
Tell us: what is the earth if not a dot?
And does not all of humanity comprise infusoria
(devour, devour yourself in a droplet of water)?

Beneath the parasol of its own atmosphere,
beneath the clouds of stupor and lies
the earth sprouts parasol souls
that will never understand the map of the Cosmos.
Their brain barely stirs a flowerbed fertilized through the ages.
The centuries of yet another deception will easily cover over
                                      a gutter of superstitions,
and once again there will be steamy vapor and fog,
and once again there will be wars and prison.
And uncountable requiems beneath the cover of a parasol –
                                      like mosquitoes over a swamp.
O humanity! O scrupulous pride!
Have you ever looked into the telescope of eternity?

    V
On the shores of eternity the sun is moving,
the sun is moving in harness-straps.
It will take on its load –
and all the planets will be in ecstasy!
Don't become bored, people, in your needs,
don't cry over petty insults.
On the shores of eternity the sun is moving,
the sun is moving in harness straps.

People, love the earth!
Poets, lead the way to the cosmos!
When there are barricades on the planets –
the universe is in pain.
On the shores of eternity the sun is moving,
the sun is moving in harness-straps.

Every planet is pregnant by the sun.
Each planet is equal and friendly to the other –
by virtue of the sun.
The orbit and the flight of each according to its strength
(the inert ones expire, powerless ones decay) –
upward – downward, upward – downward!
and echoes reverberate.

And all the systems are like communes
that took the cosmic federation's slogan –
upward – downward…

People, love the earth!
Poets, lead the way to the cosmos!
And the path to the cosmos –
is life!
On the shores of eternity the sun is moving,
the sun is moving in harness-straps.

    VI
Like a cannon ball shot from a cannon,
the earth creates its orbit around the sun.
Circling the earth in a jog, the bald moon
toothlessly looks through a monocle.

Oh, how many toothless people on earth
fear the sun and water!..
Give birth, earth, to the young at heart,
o, earth, give birth to giants!

Nations march by, they flutter in red banners:
the path – for freedom! the path – for freedom!
And with blood they will solder the earth,
and again they'll return to the earth to decay.

But to replace them – in agony
others arise accompanied by the ringing of bullets,
they drive the powers of revolutions
into a new October, a new July.[79]

Arise, you curly-headed in heart!
Arise, new republic!

---

[79] "October" signifies the second Bolshevik Revolution of 1917. Tychyna curiously uses the Russian word for October ("oktiabr'") here rather than his native Ukrainian "zhovten."

Splash out fresh ranks for us, sea!
O earth, give birth to giants!

Like a cannon ball shot from a cannon,
the earth creates its orbit around the sun.
Circling the earth in a jog, the bald moon
toothlessly looks through a monocle.

Look, look: there is no other way,
now there is no path now to the masses.
Your decades used to bloom before,
until you pitifully expired.

Be ablaze, you curly-haired in heart!
Arise, new republic!
Splash out fresh ranks for us, sea!
O earth, give birth to giants!

    VII
An anemic planet was withering in the sun
infecting the open spaces of worlds.
The sun poured handfuls of fire into the arteries of the earth.
that turned into blood.
Ah, there is always blood, in various doses,
and every struggle reflects its century –
the Last Supper.
The days of the guillotine.
Aeroplane, my soul, aeroplane,
don't lose height, don't fall.
Is it you alone who resents the human-beast,
                                the cruelty and lies?
Doesn't everyone have bullet-riddled hearts?
And thousands buried alive in the earth – are they not
        the ones who crucify your soul with a shout each night:
Oh, avenge us, avenge us. Blood for blood.
Punish whom? The sun that pours handfuls of fire
                into the arteries of the earth?

The earth that without fertilizer becomes infertile? –
Christ wasn't the first; and Robespierre won't be the last,
there is always blood in various doses,
and every struggle reflects its century.
Myriad worlds dangle the same watchwords.
The volcano of the proletariat can't halt its wrath,
and capital digs canals in a roundabout way.

I see –
Mykhailychenko and Chumak,[80] torn to pieces by teeth,
                                    and not by bayonets,
they lie in blood and look at us from a strange planet,
and the radio sends out a still warm brain:
here we, too, will meet our death –
and die for everyone –

    VIII
Humanity speaks
with three trumpeting fanfares:
Shevchenko – Whitman – Verhaeren.[81]
Like cables from nation to nation,
they powerfully dictate revolutions on the earth:
Shevchenko – Whitman – Verhaeren.

Turn on, wires,
come closer, poets,
the conscience of democracy,
the consciousness of democracy!

---

80   Ukrainian writer Hnat Mykhailychenko (1892-1919) and the poet Vasyl Chumak (1901-1919) were leftists who joined the underground to fight General Anton Denikin's Russian White Army. They were both executed on December 4, 1919.

81   Émile Verhaeren (1885-1916), Belgian socialist who sympathetically wrote about Ukraine in his poem "Praise to the Wind." Verhaeren was a humanist poet who first wrote in a naturalistic style, and was later influenced by symbolism. He often wrote anti-war poetry and poems about the brotherhood of man. Stylistically his work shares a great affinity with Whitman.

Let the blind minstrels play the "Last Judgment" on their lyres
                for the Cossack scalplock and riding pants – [82]
our last judgment has come.
(Above us the shadow of a cherubim –
a blessed path! –
Such incomprehensible music! –
propellers hum...)
Our last judgment has come.
It is he who has cast a furrow that you'll be plowing forever.
It is he who spit into the Dnipro
and parted it in two.
(Above us the shadow of a cherubim –
a blessed path! –
Such incomprehensible music! –
propellers hum...)
Cannons strike and all the corners of the earth detonate.
Continents split and kingdoms fall apart,
and storms, like *surmas*,[83] are over the cemetery of peoples.
Sonorous oboes, genies of the caves, poets on the ridge,
merge your voice with the voice of *surmas*!
Humanity speaks
with three trumpeting fanfares:
Shevchenko – Whitman – Verhaeren.

    IX
Once the gardens of Semiramis[84] bloomed,
and one hundred and twenty brooks branched from the Nile,
supplying water to the field and mountain,
making rain for the weary queen.
And all of this with the hands of slaves.
The hands of slaves...

---

82   "Sharovary" – are loose and baggy pants that Ukrainian Cossacks wore. The style of dress was borrowed from the Turks, one of the main enemies of the Cossacks.

83   See note #65.

84   The daughter of the goddess Derceto (or Derketo) who was nurtured by doves. After the death of her husband Ninus, Semiramis became queen of Nineva. The founding of Babylon and the Hanging Gardens have been attributed to her.

Then why are we an accursed generation,
why are we unable to come together,
to begin work
and renew the land?

(Stand together closer, those strong of heart,
beneath a single banner!)
Is our yoke eternal?
Along with tsars, prisons and oppression?
As well as exhaustion, submission,
and the convict's brand?

Who, who are those, who began to laugh in Europe,
who began to wail
that here we're dying of hunger
but won't surrender to our enemies?
(Stand closer together, those strong of heart,
beneath a single banner!)
Yes, yes, we're bloating without bread.
Our hope – the children – are dying.
But hunger is the language of the revolution.
And what if the workers of the world
clout you from behind your back? –
Who, who are those, who began to laugh in Europe,
who began to wail
that here we're dying of hunger
but won't surrender to our enemies?

    X
In tsars they found their guardians and kin,
in the bourgeoisie their own peace, sloth, and sleep...
It is you who duped the Republic with lies
and unscrupulously escaped abroad.
Boundaries, stakes, and knives were mixed in blood:
for land, for everything "native," for their own...
To foreigners you're ridiculous, you're foreign to your own masses.
it is at you, walking abortions, that time spits in the face.

In Europe, in that tavern, to the derision of all, to shame,
you diplomatize elegantly – the wine swirls...
And you measure the fertile steppe like merchandise,
for epaulettes, for subsidies, for a word of praise...

Do you have hope? For darkness, for the superstitions of the masses?
From where do those rivers come that rend yours dams! –
Who yearns – to see the unembellished truth,
to comprehend the law of life, to create a life without shackles!

You still have hope? So perish, die like dogs in taverns,
so your bones putrefy and become moldy!..
Why did you dupe the ignorant and blind?
Why did you set brother against brother?

Put on your beggar's sack and extend your hand, –
still, maybe, you'll find a stupid little tsar
who'll come to save you, to strangle the people,
and to liberate you for a savory tidbit.

Put on your beggar's sack – maybe someone will give you a handout,
maybe someone will cry with you, and will remember and sigh
about how you once used to live, about how you bought power,
and how you reek now of an unbearably rotten corpse...

Have hope... Intoxicate yourself with your lies,
we'll move forward – history won't wait.
Proletarians! Call to each other in the struggle –
The Inter-Republic, the Republic's approaching!

1921

WIND FROM UKRAINE
(1924)

WIND FROM UKRAINE

To Mykola Khvylovyi[85]

I love no one
as much as the whipping wind.

Infernal wind! Accursed wind!

It will lift up its hand to strike.
                howling! whistling! swirling!
dead leaves in the grove
are already like the devil's seed...

Or: it will take root in the muddy field,
it will boost the power of train cars.
oh, when they rush along the rails
even the poplars will bend!..

Infernal wind! Accursed wind!

Rabindranath[86] sits in Bengalia:
there's no spirit of rebellion among us: man is just clay. –
The wind from Ukraine is roaring with laughter,
the wind from Ukraine!

Through lenses the West peers as if through gratings:
is this the march of a beast or that of a man? –
The wind from Ukraine is roaring with laughter,
the wind from Ukraine!

---

85   (1893-1933). His real last name was Fitilov. The great Ukrainian prose writer and proponent of Romantic Vitalism and a mandate to look toward the west for literary models rather than to Russia. He later committed suicide in 1933 after Stalin's vicious crackdown against Ukrainian intellectuals. For a selection of his works in translation see: *Stories from the Ukraine*, Trans. George S.N. Luckyj (New York: Philosophical Library, 1960).

86   Rabindranath Tagore (1861-1941), Indian writer and philosopher whose works were extraordinarily popular in Russia and Ukraine.

Infernal wind! Accursed wind!

It raises its bushy head from the Dnipro:
don't expect anything good from it, gentlemen:
the game is futile!
Ah,
I love no one
as much as the whipping wind.
its paths, its aching pain
and the land,
this land of mine.

April 18, 1923

YAROSLAVNA'S LAMENT[87]

I

For Lida Paparuk[88]

Snow. More snow.
Onto the royal tower.
Day and night she paces around it,
her feeble voice laments:
    "O prince, my prince,
    be you beyond the Danube?
    be you on the River Don?
    Oh, give me news of your fate,
    for I will surely die."
The princess listens – but there is only snow,
    only snow all around,
    and beyond the field and the forest
    the voice of hunger speaks:
        Father's at war!
        Mother's no more!
        Who'll plow the land, who'll sow the seed?
        O-oh-woe!

Oh, what desolation.

Here the princess begins again:
"Serve me, sail,
you black-browed wind!"
    Somewhere the prince is sounding a retreat
    with a handful of his retinue.
    turn the arrows away from him,

---

[87] Yaroslavna was the wife of Prince Ihor (Igor.in Russian) who was captured in a campaign against the Polovtsian tribe in the late 12th century. His capture and subsequent events are the subject of the epic *The Lay of the Host of Ihor/Igor*.

[88] Tychyna's wife (1900-1975), whom he met in 1916 when he was a lodger at her family's house while he was attending classes at the Commercial Institute in Kyiv.

send them back.
The princess listens closely – but there is no wind,
    just snow and winter,
    and beyond the field and forest
    she hears voices:
        We'll turn you back!
        We'll send you off alone!
        You'll lay your body down like your prince.
        like a stone...

Oh, what desolation.

"Dnipro, Dnipro, dream-sleeper,
You're father to us all.
At least you must rise up – even without your prince.
to restore the kingdom.
    A quiet kingdom, a righteous one,
    one so wise in its laws:
    so that some can tend to the land,
    and others to the crown.
The princess listens closely – just laughter,
    it's just laughter shaking,
    and the rumbling louder, quaking
    from under huts and thatched roofs.
        Has the prince returned from the campaign?
        Has his retinue come back?
The princess listens closely – the clash of sabers and a salvo,
    and the voices come even closer:
    We'll restore you!"

Oh, what desolation.

II

A strange flotilla glistens in the sun,
shaking the heavens with a hymn,
playing its wing.
They are the titans

of the black earth returning.
From a faraway fairy-tale land,
yonder, where the kings are.

The faraway fairy-tale land
killed the lord and master,
but not those
who have iron blood flowing
in their young veins,
who have sun-sprinkling song
and genuine laughter.

What is it rustling-ringing in the hills?
What is it shaking the dust
in the morning at dawn?
It is kings and tsars running away
fouling things up on their way.
Following them everywhere,
the workers become chiefs.

Above the hills, over the steppe
they've scattered in a threatening chain,
they've formed a single choir.
Don't hide, sly foxes,
we'll pull you out from your burrows!
They're striking from above, flinging flashes of light.
only a motor is rumbling...

A strange flotilla glistens on the sun,
shaking the heavens with a hymn,
playing its wing.
These are the titans of the black earth
returning.
From a faraway fairy-tale land,
yonder, where the kings are.

Ladas[89] meet them below,
and also the full range
of the recent disarray.
Like a woman – slim and cradlerocking.
a wheat field is grainfilling.
Farther than the sea, like an overripe sheaf of wheat
she's dangling and rustling...

1923

---

89   Lada, besides being a fairly common female Ukrainian name today, was an ancient Slavic goddess of love.

SUMMER'S ON THE WAY...

Summer's on the way,
do you feel it – on the way? –
The grove becomes swoony. The river slender.
In the orchards blossoms are falling...
The sky is lush. The days aren't quite the same.
The distance is growing abundant. And beyond the
barnyards a raspberry bush's eyelashes turn gray...
The distance is growing abundant.

On a clay bench an aged grandpa
sitting like a dream.
His grandson tousles his eyebrows.
The wind sways poppies, poppies and sycamore maples.
The son
sticks his shovel into the ground
and goes to the house. How warm it is!
In a week or so the rye-fields will really
begin to glisten beneath the clear sky.

We've survived wars and misfortune,
we've liberated the young land
and divided it up. The rest of it is still to be
divided – then it will all be done.
Silence. Someone in the area hears a commotion and rumble.
Someone is driving through the street. Silence.
In a week or so the earth will really
begin to glisten beneath the clear sky.

The neighboring village brought in electricity.
Isn't it our turn? Grandpa shakes his head.
A well creaks behind the house.
The still standing timber
is trembling and dangling, look – it's falling.
We'll have an artesian well, we'll survive!
Grandpa shakes his head.

And above the village a prankster-plane
nonchalantly outlines the plan with his wings.

A happy young mother comes out of the house,
asking: where's my son?
A child with these hands, a child with these feet – what a lad!
For sure he'll be Komsomol[90] kid – don't you think?
And now he is in her arms.
He's forgotten grandpa, he's forgotten it all,
half shutting his eyes he suckles her breast...
Summer is on the way.

1924

---

90   The Communist Youth League, an organization for the political indoctrination of young people in the former USSR.

MYKYTA THE TANNER[91]

Mykyta was tanning hides.
when people came to him,
in tears:
"O, woe, Mykyta, if only you knew,
such woe, if only you knew!

A dragon-king
has surrounded the city.
what will you say to him?
I'll show mercy after I drink up your blood.
what can you say to him?"

Anger overcame Mykyta.
he didn't raise his head,
he tore twelve hides with his bare hands,
he just tore them to shreds!

They came to him a second time:
each one with his nose cut off,
with no ears,
without lips.
And they started to whine shrilly:
"O, woe, Mykyta, if only you knew,
such woe, if only you knew!"

---

91   Mykyta Kozhumiaka, whose surname means "tanner," or literally "one who makes leather soft," is a *bohatyr*, one of the heroes of Ukrainian fairy tales and folklore. In the Ukrainian version of the fairy tale, Kyrylo Kozhumiaka agrees to fight a dragon to save a princess after children, the third party to make the request of him, bring him to tears with their plea. After defeating the dragon in battle, Kyrylo asks for nothing in return for his good deed, and the Prince as a reward names the spot where Kyrylo lives in Kyiv .Kozhumiake. (Tanner's Place). The tale also appears in Aleksandr Afanas'ev's famous collection of Russian and Slavic folk tales under the title "Nikita Kozhemiaka." Nikita is the Russian form of the Ukrainian first name Mykyta. The tale is available in English translation as "Kirilo the Tanner" in *Ukrainian Folk Tales* (Kyiv: Dnipro, 1981): 155-7.

Pity overcame Mykyta—
he called them fools:
fools, stupid fools,
when will they finally become extinct!

And a third time they came to him:
and each one held before him:
a headless wife,
a headless son,
with their legs ambling so horrifyingly, ridiculously.
as if they were still alive...

Here Mykyta abruptly rose and vented.
You're all headless!
What will come of it if I help you?
Three times you've come, three times you've been the same.
what fools you are!
Where are your champions?

Ah! – echoed – and silence reigned.
Their eyes gaped – and silence reigned.

"Why are their ears not cut off?"
"Why have their sons not been butchered?"

Ah! – they arose – and silence reigned.
Their eyes agape – and they all conjectured.
(the blood of the dead glistened while they ran)...

They heaped the dead on a pile.
The living stood up separately.
They've struck upon a champion!
Mykyta against the king!

And the very earth began to seethe...

1924

THREE SONS

Three sons came to their mother,
three warriors, each one different from the other.
    One fought for the poor,
      the second for the wealthy,
the third, with nowhere to use his power –
    is simply a bandit.

"Oh, Momma!" says the first hazel-eyed one,
"it's a great wide world out there!
We're not the only ones who battle with misery,
We're not the only ones burdened by misfortune,
beyond the sea people suffer in the very same way,
for the accursed rich are everywhere."

"Oh, Mom!" says the second dark-skinned one,[92]
"why should we think about the far-off world,
when we have everything from nature:
grain, coal, and the boughs of trees.
Let the foreign, the alien, and the hated
be hung by the neck on these boughs."

---

92   Literally "chornohrekyi" would be: black-Greek, i.e., as dark-skinned as a Greek.

"Oh, Mother!" says the third low-browed one,
"chase your sons out of the house,
so they don't look ridiculous or anger me.
            A big strong fist –
that is freedom, brotherhood, and the happiness of the land:
I don't distinguish between rich or poor."

The first one's saber flashed!
The second one's saber sparked a fire,
And the third one's dagger...
"Oh, son, my darling son!"
The bandit's lying dead,
And the two brothers took up their fight again –
no one can pry them apart.

1923

FAUST IS WALKING...

Faust is walking through Europe
through sneers, whistles, and rumors –
a prayer book in his hands,
he is contemplating this and that
when Prometheus approaches it.

Hello, hi there, Prometheus!
Ah! You're rebelling? – go on, then, rebel.
I can't heap praise on you:
ah, with revolts, you're rebelling,
planning to make the poor happy?

I know the secrets of the heavens,
I love philosophy,
I toss around numbers in my mind,
the facts of deaths and misery –
and you, and you, what do you do?

I carry chains in my soul,
I shun no religions,
I don't revolt – but just write
book after book.
and you, and you, what do you do?

You want to create a new world?
Then why don't you have a job?
"Because you're not Faust!
Because you're a petty squire!
Just watch me take up my hammer!"

Ah! You're rebelling? – I see, I see.
I'm not Faust? – that doesn't surprise me.
Well, forgive me then! Good-bye!
Faust is walking through Europe
with a prayer book in his hands.

March 12, 1923

FAMINE[93]

If only the sun would rise... "Mommy, some bread!"
Her father got up: "shut up!"
Near the fire in the train car starving refugees
huddle together, dying.

Smoke devours their eyes.
Cold penetrates to the bone.
And behind the train car shouts and a racket,
a barter, a deal, and whistles.

A mother bent over in rags,
in sorrow, in sores. She bundled up
her child in something: "go to sleep, go to sleep." –
"may you go to sleep forever..." Life!

We came here, but the famine followed.
But there are no people among the people.
Have you heard?.. nearby a woman recently
cooked her two children...

The father recoiled: "you've gone insane!" –
"shut up! shut up! What do you mean by that?"
The mother sprang up and shrieked,
and father spit in her face...

1921

---

93   A famine that took the lives of several hundred thousand peasants swept through Ukraine in 1921-2 following the unsuccessful war for independence from the Bolsheviks. It was caused by a combination of grain confiscation by the new Bolshevik regime, high taxes on individual farmers that resulted in a stoppage of production by peasants, and a natural disaster – a drought in southern Russia and Ukraine. Relief efforts eased the impact of the famine by 1922.

AN ANSWER TO MY COUNTRYMEN

> ...this poet for several years has been kissing
> the slipper of the Pope.[94]
> –*From foreign newspapers*

Like Dante in hell,
I stand among bandits and criminals,
among the fat-guts, the gorged, the mercenaries,
among the trifling, the vengeful, the dimwitted,
on a pile of bilious manure that sucks everything to the bottom:
sing, poet, sing with us in tune!

I stand firm – like a cliff.

And they swarm around me
in mire, in mud, the way serpents
entangle themselves in a ball and fall,
and thick mud covers their mouths...
And they,
apparently drunk, prattle something,
extend their hand to me and claw at my clothing.
O, be damned all of you – I don't know you!
Don't touch me, don't howl!
Your own swamp – you said.
here are the doors to heaven,
but secretly you thought: let it be so,
just give us a chance to grow up,
we'll still show them who we are.
Poets and nations will go with us.

---

94   Part of the concluding lines of Tychyna's collection *Instead of Sonnets and Octaves.*

There will be no feuds, no evil,
when instead of bloody banners
everyone overhead will see
his own eagle with a pointed beak...[95]
So on they went. Got mired in the mud. Got lost.
They choked in pogroms. Got drunk...
O, be damned again!
You won't buy my soul
with laurel wreaths,
or with gold, or with bread, or with an eagle medal.

I stand firm – like a cliff.

1922

---

95 The eagle is the emblem of tsarist Russia as well as the traditional emblem of Poland.

I WILL SPEAK FOR ALL...

I will speak for all and suffer for everyone,
Walking every minute to answer, to be judged.
I will not drown in the depths or grow shallower,
I grow with wings spread in the summits.

Never before has my soul been so courageous!
Never before has my spirit grown so fervent!
O lucid spirit – without poison or sting.
how long since you've been dreaming? – and here the day's action

has embraced all of me, squeezed me, stretched me,
and I arise, I inhale a new strength.
I don't dream, no, I've opened my eyes forever.
irony and pride on my face,
irony...

> Why should I care, colleagues,
> whether I'm the first poet or the last?
> Put on your crowns and go,
> open your mouths...
>
> Why should I care, colleagues,
> whether I'm a late or early forerunner?
> pretend You're prophets and go,
> open your mouths...
>
> There behind me, behind me, behind me,
> I don't know how many, there are so many walking!
> The new day comes before me
> at a steady pace.
>
> There behind me, behind me, behind me,
> both the plow and the run-down machines.
> Before me a joyful sea,
> a sea of heads...

Where will I go after this,
and how can I look back at you,
when the sun pierces my mind,
and the sun my lips?

I've reached my height and strength,
I've seen the light in the distance.
Why should I care, dear friends,
whether or not I'm the first?

1922

O STRENGTH OF MY HATE...[96]

O strength of my hate,
O depth of my love,
how hard it is to carry you in my heart,
how hard it is for me again.

Again and again foam floats up
onto the superficialities of time...
To whom should I bring
my pure soul?

Once again dullness, hypocrisy,
extortion, deceit, and lies.
Only the minority[97] has not been extinguished
without changing its banners.

Only the minority is certain of the goal,
everywhere, at all times and ages.
O people, people, don't lock up
your souls!

---

96   Later republications of this poem had the following subtitle, which gave it a propagandist bent: "(During the days after the death of V. I. Lenin)."

97   *Menshist* in the Ukrainian suggests "Mensheviks," or minority party, as opposed to the Bolsheviks, the majority party. In an irony of appellation, the Bolsheviks were actually in the minority.

O people, paper souls,
can I reach you and light up a spark?
When can I overcome your emptiness
with fire?

I wouldn't scream so, I wouldn't call out.
but you can't stifle a shout.
For our supreme titan[98]
has already gone, has already gone away...

1924

---

98 *Holovnyi titan* (chief, supreme titan) refers to Vladimir Lenin, who died on January 21, 1924.

TO GREAT LIARS
(An answer to some people)

"Oh, how we so love harmony!"
We want to see the world translucent, not opaque.
Life for us is but sound, a sleepy, tonal trance,
and the working class like perpetual dissonance.

We see peace where there are battles and storms:
we see beauty in death, and truth in a pun.
And we clang against hearts, and cry over the fact
that all this is dust and rust, the vapor of demented blood.

So, how do we break the prison gratings of tyrants,
when all our bards are eunuchs and castrates?
"Chains are a sign, and gratings a chord.
Radiance from an ass. And peace from lion snouts..."

Harmony lives not only in patches of sunlight.
Among Great Liars there is also harmony.
Only the liars will die, but truth from century to century
will flow into a single chord, where the worker is sound.

1922

BEFORE A MONUMENT TO PUSHKIN IN ODESSA

Take care, my Pushkin, mighty organ of the earth!
And you, the sea's depth, and you, Odessa clouds!
I'm a guest here with you, and I'm glad to see you all.
Don't be angry at my laughter: I'm still so young.

A husked boulevard. Puddles bubble in a muddy suspension.
And Pushkin on a pillar – swims into the grime as though into a harbor.
Where are you going, wait! – he doesn't want to speak.
Below the howl of a siren, and the sea surges.

It's the grateful sons of an ungrateful Russia who
erected him... with his back to the forces of nature.
Stand sideways to the people, to the multitudinous squares;
the Lord will forgive the poems and even the downpour of epigrams...

Ah, the sea and the poet! Who doesn't fear you!
The black wrath of freedom. The luster, the tempering, the steel.
It's good to be a poet: when you die – they install you sideways,
turned away from freedom, so the people won't be able to recognize you.

1920

SUCH A LOVELY AUTUMN...

Such a lovely autumn,
an autumn,
so splendid.
Autumn brings food to mommy:
 borsht in a pot,
 kasha in her hand,
 a slice of bread in her blouse,
 pears in her apron.

Such a lovely autumn,
an autumn,
so splendid.
She'll come, set it down: "Mom, are you sleeping?"
 Mother lifts herself up:
 "Is it you, my daughter?"
 "I took a stroll through the forest,
 an oak tree tried to snatch my kerchief,
 he wanted to catch up to me,
 to take away the borsht!"

Such a lovely autumn,
an autumn,
so splendid.
"Mom, Mom, Mommy, why aren't you eating?"
 Momma's eyes
 glanced quickly,
 her body slid to the ground,
 her arm slung down...
 Such a lovely autumn,
an autumn,
so splendid.
"Mom, Mom, Mommy, why aren't you eating?"

1921

ON A FARMSTEAD

...A little girl on a clay bench:
cheep-cheep-cheep!..
A dog on a chain.
Something's buzzing in the steppe.

Her mother runs from the garden.
something's buzzing in the steppe.
"O, my world, it's a storm coming!"
something's buzzing in the steppe.

"No, Momma, it's not a storm,"
I read about it: "it's a squadron."
Mother trembles from terror,
the livestock bellows in the pen...

And the sky swirled
in several hundred circles,
and then returned,
and the buzzing grew distant.

– the buzzing grew distant –

1924

WE SAY...

We say: the sun is rising
     But it's like this:
In the morning
a little girl, Red Riding Hood.
wakes up...
She washes up or not.
grabs a basket and sets off to the dark blue woods!

But in the woods, it's hot!..
Storm clouds before the rain
like a pack of dogs:
they scratch behind their ears,
and their teeth chatter! chatter!

In the woods it's sticky, and here comes a wolf (the moon):
where are you going, anyway?
"From the east all the way to the west,
because my family lives there,
they keep waiting for Little Red Riding Hood."

"What if I eat you?" "Try."
Little Red Riding Hood grabs her knife!
She aimed at the wolf's bald head,
and hurries up to where
they keep waiting and waiting for her.

We say: the sun is setting.

1922

SPRING
(From Baratynsky)[99]

Spring, spring! Such azure blue,
such translucence all around!
Bloombuds move through the gardens
with goldenvoyance in the sky.[100]

Spring, spring! What dash is there
on the wings of the breeze?.
floating-dissolving in the heights,
that's cloud-cloudy river.

The foam froth-makers roar above;
and, on its back, the river
majestically carries forward
its playful, thawing bits.

The deep blue forest hasn't yet turned green,
but the sprouting flowers
have already lifted and separated
last year's decaying leaves.

And there in the high depth,

---

[99] Russian pre-romantic poet Evgeny Baratynsky (1800-1844), who devoted a number of his lyrical works to nature, especially to spring. This poem is an imitation of Baratynsky's poem 'Vesna, vesna! kak vozdukh chist.... (Spring, spring! How pure the air is...; 1834). Tychyna's poem began as a translation of Baratynsky, but evolved so much that Tychyna eventually regarded it as an original poem and included it in his collection.

[100] *Brun'kotsvit* is one of Tychyna's neologisms. It comes from the combination of *brun'ka* (bud) and *tsvit* (bloom). I translate it as "bloombuds" here. *Zlotozor* consists of the word *z(o)loto* (gold/en) and the root *zor* (meaning sight), for which I've created a neologism in English – "goldenvoyance."

where the clear skytone[101] sinks,
a mother-of-pearl lark entones:[102]
cloud-cloudy spring!

1921

---

101   *Ton'* is one of Tychyna's virtually untranslatable neologisms. It suggests both the aural meaning of tone as well as the color of the sky.

102   The neologism *tonyt'* is a verbalized third person singular form of the neologism *ton'*, which is discussed in the immediately preceding note. Tychyna stresses sound in the verbal form.

LA BELLA FORNARINA

Along the Tibrus Raphael floated
In evening time in June.
"This sorrow, this dream, I lullingly stream,
Lulling I lulla swoon."

His heart beat fast. He listened closely:
Oh, how she can sing!
"Whether he loves or not, she wrings her hands,
and he moors in a cove."

The song draws near. From behind the trees
a beautiful dove fluttered out.
O, who are you, girl, tell me please!
she (shyly) said: Fornarina.

And Raphael took her by the hand,
She uttered not a tone.
She burst into tears. And he embraced her:
calling her: My Madonna!

1921

STORM CLOUDS LAY ALL AROUND...
A hexameter

Storm clouds lay a siege everywhere – and the field hid into shadow.
The cheerful birds grew silent. The grass turned silent and shriveled.
Only the birch trees grieved. Behind them willows swayed.
The wind flitted from a grove flying past on dust-covered paths,
like a horse that bolts up escaping from a fire. Far away!
He's already run far, and for the raven-colored one, it seems:
a giant is chasing after him, releasing manes of fire.
Thus that furious wind, messenger of thunderous wrath and rain,
ran to the ravines, and exhausted, fell the ground.
At his heels, from the grove, tiny red leaves
were flung and began to play in a whirlwind, fusing together
                                              as though in a dance.
The fluttering continued for a while, playing softly with the silence.
upward, upward, until heavy droplets splattered,
and the roar began to approach. It slashed along the clouds and fizzled!
Then a pure gold shimmer surged downward.
lower and lower it settled, fusing together as though in a dance.
And turning around for the last time, each one of them lay down
                                              on the ground,
each one in its place, as though to eternal sleep.
Once again it flashed – a chesty laugh thundered from somewhere
                                              in the mountains!
It cracked, it shook, it quieted down... Only the roaring
                                              continued to roar,
a roaring, to which you could listen forever.
                                  The day turned fresh and clear...

1921

THE REBELS
(A Fragment)

"Well, have you rested up?" "Onward!" It's time, friends, for the road!
Konetspolsky's[103] already waiting somewhere, time to act,
                              not let our hair go gray."
The *otaman*[104] shouted to the grove: "To your horses, Cossacks,
                              to your horses!"
His shout swept through the forest and passed from wagon to wagon,
gushing down like rainy dew, somewhere far off it tumbled down
                              in thunder...
The rebels bustled, came out – making the forest rustle in the treetops.
He who rides first, flies like a falcon,
the newly chosen *otaman* on a swift black horse.
A mass of rebels behind him! — here and there they set up ranks,
marching in line, pushing forward, if you look back
                              – you can't see the end:
one behind the other – all on horseback, one behind the other, singing.
Far off in the distance a supply column bent like a snake along the road.
The throng arose for a righteous cause, for honor, and for their land.
The Poles are billeted – there's no order or way to get through.
Ukraine will suffer, until the masses strike.
Until they thrash the Poles and send them to the netherworld!
They'll violently rock them like Triasylo[105] once did in Korsun!
The rebels ride on and laugh – here and there they set up ranks,
one after the other — all on horseback, one after the other,
                              continuing to sing.
Suddenly the *otaman* halts. Far off above the road

---

103   Stanislav Konetspolsky (1591-1646), a hetman in collusion with the Polish crown who supported Polish expansion into Ukrainian lands. He headed a Polish army that viciously suppressed Cossack insurrections.

104   The elected leader of a Cossack regiment or company.

105   Taras Triasylo, hetman of the Zaporozhian Cossacks who were not registered with the Polish crown. He led an uprising against Konetspolsky in March 1630 at the city of Korsun. While other Cossack leaders compromised with Konetspolsky to end the battle, Triasylo refused and returned to his home camp on the River Dnipro. Taras Shevchenko devoted his poem "Tarasova nich" (The Night of Taras) to the battle.

         something can be seen.
It can be seen, it's growing, becoming restive,
       like a poppy in the field before dawn.
"Brothers!" the *otaman* speaks. "We've sat out a storm in the forest;
put away your pipes – and we'll still greet this storm in the open field.
You move aside right away. And you go into that ravine.
We'll pitch camp here. Let the supply column get closer."
Just as he said it, it was done, and the poppies
        keep blooming, approaching,
coming closer and spreading, increasing the stamping of hooves...
They stopped. They veiled themselves with smoke –
       and aim at the supply column again.
The *otaman* himself took a shot – and a Pole teetered on his horse.
Then they took a shot together – after which, yet two more fell.
Oh, how the Poles move forward, how they fling themselves like beasts,
you can't see the ground! they'll sweep you up, then knock you down.
But the rebels didn't waste time, they circled behind,
       running off to the side,
then those whom the valley was hiding came out to attack.
Come on, stand together, Poles, forget all the roads back!
One storm cloud covered another, as though the sun
       hadn't risen since night.
And here the rifles grew silent: they rose up to slash each other, to fight.
The earth's throat grew hoarse, the ground became
       bloodstained and scorched black.
And only their sabers were clashing, and their eyes were like a wolf's.
A shout or a neigh would spurt out and get lost in the din.
The savagery lasted for a while, until everyone was hacked to pieces.
The sabers fell from their hands. "Maybe this is enough?"
       The *otaman* halted.
In silence they gathered together, wiping their sabers
       and breathing heavily.
In silence the flowering field lay flat all around.
Enough! It's apparently as it ought to be. We've put the accursed nobles
to shameful sleep. They will not rise. They will not return.
       Bury your men.

Just as he said it, it was done. They heaped a high mound

in the field, they buried their brothers in it, forever.
The rebels set off and left – from far away you can see the burial mound.
The evening above it was inconsolable and the burial cloth over it fresh.

1921

CLEON AND DIODOT[106]

There's a stirring and anxiety in Athens, the Athenians
                                                    convened a council.
The patricians of Myletia will be there! They're discussing independence!
To betray us at such a moment when our army is on a campaign...
Let's cut off their heads right here, why prattle with them?
Quiet, men, hold still: it's time for us to convene a council.
There, the war leaders are coming, behind them the Myletian delegation.
The Athenians began to clamor, as though they were conjuring a storm,
readying to ravage or to prepare provisions for a campaign,
for a long time they cursed, attacking one other,
                                                    splitting into two camps.
Here Cleon the son of Cleenet stepped out, a brazen man
                                                    well-known to all,
in the past assembly he had favored the penalty of death,
The Athenians quieted the clamor, and quickly grew completely silent.
Casting his eye around, he began to speak:
"several times I've said it, and today I'll say it again:
a democratic country is incapable of ruling.
Somehow it doesn't know how to put a bridle on other nations.
Of this I'm convinced. To what end have we lived? Have the Athenians
forgotten the judgment of yesterday? Should we believe the Myletians?
Again I'll remind you: we should rule by tyranny.
As soon as we relax, our allies will stop obeying us;
they and others will rise against us using the example of these Myletians.
It is better to have laws that are bad, as long as they are immutable,
it is better to be uneducated rather than have a learnedness that enslaves!
What good are these marvelous laws, when it is silly to abide by them?
Are we here going to decide – to change our minds?
                                                    Athenians, more simply:

---

106   Cleon (d. 422 BC), the demagogic and imperialist Athenian politician and son of a tanner, the first of the commercial class to assume power in the city state. He ascended to power after the death of Pericles in 429. Known for his brutality against rebellious populations in subject states, in 427 he ordered the men of Mytilene on the island of Lesbos to be killed and their women and children enslaved. The order was later overturned. Aristophanes viciously attacks him in the play *The Knights*.

the Myletians have betrayed us, they've dealt us a great insult,
what next, do we punish them or do we permit a benevolent tear?
I advise you not to think long. I'll not say another word."
As he stepped down, the crowd surged like waves in the sea.
A clamor rushed through like the wind and suddenly
                    broke loose everywhere.
The Athenians created an uproar, splitting into two camps.
For a long time they cursed, going at each other,
                    until a new speaker stepped out.
It was Diodot, the son of Euchrates, who formerly
                    had been against the punishment.
The Athenians muted the uproar, and it soon completely quieted down.
Casting his eye all around, he began to speak:
"I'm speaking out not to contradict Cleon,
I'm speaking out not to judge the Myletians.
the question here is not about a crime, but about our sobermindedness.
Why should we provoke the assembly and carry out a hasty judgment?
The present has blinded you, but I've become accustomed
                    to look to the future.
Will the rebellions decrease if we punish the Myletians?
People grow accustomed to anything, they'll even get used to death.
All the more they'll grow accustomed if misery forces them.
Will we then think up a punishment more cruel than death?
Is the harshness of laws all of which our nation is capable?
No, harshness is not the law for us, but our wisdom, Athenians!
Why should we exploit those who united with us as equals?
Right now, in neighboring nations, only one party is in power.
this is a democratic party, and it is in contact with us.
Should we destroy all the Myletians? Should we summon hate upon us?
I advise you to think about this. I'll not say another word."

As he stepped down, the crowd swayed like waves in the sea.
A clamor rushed through like the wind and suddenly
                    broke loose everywhere.
The Athenians created an uproar, splitting into two camps.
Be silent, men, there's no need: it is time to begin the vote.
"Be silent!" – the war leaders shouted, and
                    the emissaries of the Myletians grew pale.

This is the way the flooding of the sea recedes protractedly after a storm.
For a while, all around, they swayed and grew pale,
                            and touched their hearts...
The Athenians muted the uproar, and it soon grew completely silent.
The majority voted against punishment. Diodot was overjoyed.

1921

FROM MY DIARY

I

Oh, storm clouds, storm clouds from the German lands! It's you who caused such a din: you who gave the River Dnipro a hetman's mace.[107] The Dnipro twisted it this way and that, and, for a long time, admired it. This is how we'll shake the Hetmanate! A wondrous dream has been realized! – The worker laughed at first, and then became troubled...

They've made a throne, offered a mass of supplication, and did all manner of things. Dnipro, of course, danced a *hopak*.[108] A hundred hundreds of German dogs, and just as many from the Don, sat in epaulettes around the throne and began to snarl at people. And the all-Russian ideas began to smell like relics. At first people endured, and then...

Oh, storm clouds, storm clouds from the German lands!

1918

II

"The Dnipro is a bandit." You can find everything in this phrase. Foreign oppression, and hate, our own feebleness, and despair.

It's a May that's not like May. The summer has not gotten its fill of sleep, and autumn is here already.

How can it be: are the people who took off the rusted shackles struck with rust as if with an illness? How can it be: has the lofty spirit squandered itself in public and degenerated? Is it not the spirit of Siberia above us? Have we not caught sight of the tsarist biers? Ah! From the White Sea do I sense the incense of the Solovetsky Monastery?[109] Chimes and obscenities commingled in it, banditry and freedom. And

---

107   The mace was the Cossack hetman's symbol of power. The German-controlled Hetmanate took over the Ukrainian government in 1918.

108   An extraordinarily fast Ukrainian dance marked by various jumps and gyrations.

109   A monastery to which Ivan the Terrible often retreated.

Ivan the IVth the Terrible, having impaled the leg of a smelly dog with an iron staff, stands, and listens, and fingers his rosary beads...
1919 During the time of Denikin[110]

III

With blue tears the lake cries profusely. Above it – the sky: "don't cry!" – it says, but it can not stop its sobbing: cloud after cloud tears the soulapart. Cloud after cloud. On the shore – geese. Like snow. Geese – "a snowy fluttering" – I say. "why don't you stop the wind?.." A garden stands below and rehearses the song of autumn. The wind runs up to the walnut trees – the walnuts drop their yellowed notes, not knowing how to sing; the wind rushes to the acacias – but the acacias are already rushing too swiftly. The weeds cry out: and how about me? and me? But the wind grew angry: you've all forgotten how to sing! And already it's beyond the village, beyond the village of Lystopadove,[111] 27 and the mills have the last say – "into a circle! into a circle!" And the weeds call after it: "my dear, what about me?"

With blue tears the lake cries profusely. And only from time to time a wave from the opposite direction will sprinkle it with sand. With the red one? – Along the deep blue...

Geese on the shore.

1920 With the Stetsenko Chorus on tour in Ukraine.
The village of Zlatopil, on a hill

---

110   General Anton Denikin, leader of the anti-Bolshevik southern White Volunteer Army troops in the Civil War, which began in the summer of 1918 and lasted until the end of 1920.

111   The village's name means "November," with the Ukrainian word for the month coming from the words *lyst* (leaf) and *pad* (falling) with the linking vowel "o."

WE LIVE AS A COMMUNE

I

We live as a commune, we work. Amid the mountains, a monastery. All around a forest, and before us the river Dnipro itself. It's sort of strange – not easy to recognize at once. It continues to slumber, to think, we'll never cease dreaming. We live as a commune, we work.

At the crack of dawn – with spades we go to the monastery field. The monks silently pass us and for a long time cross themselves and spit to the right and to the left. A noisy gong calls to breakfast. To greet us the sun pours out its hymn… We laugh, we have faith, we're aflame! Only the Dnipro grows all the more somber. He continues to muse, he will never get enough of dreaming.

II

Yellow butterflies are over the cabbage patch, and over the Dnipro. white ones.

Sails strain their breasts, oars sparkle in the sun, paths glisten behind the skiffs – and only a song carries over the water: "Oh, quack, quack, little geese, to the pond."

Yellow butterflies are over the cabbage patch, and over the Dnipro. white ones.

The barges float and carry wood, some of it cut, some still untouched. The hungry city will swallow everything but will freeze anyway.

Then: "at least give something to the worker!" They're laughing: "we'll give some to everyone! Here we've come for the winter as brigade commanders, so maybe, we'll put an end to you."

Oh, no! you won't see that! No way!

Oh, quack, quack, little geese, to the pond.

III

At night we dream of phalanxes, of farming. And during the day we stumble on blood. The village is in a frenzy – we had to defend ourselves. We've gotten used to the blood a long time ago, though we don't glorify it in our canon. At night we dream of phalanxes, of farming.

A wounded man: "You took away the peace from us that you'll never return. You've cast away God and robbed the land – may you be damned!"

We took him, nursed him, taught him to read and write, and opened up a curtain before his eyes. And now he's ours. He works in the field with us, in the theater he ripens in spirit and knows, that not everyone has red blood. We've gotten used to blood a long time ago, although we don't glorify it in our canon.

IV

We still don't have enough music. And everyone's heart is deaf. Each person still has a wife to calls his own. And children don't want to leave their mothers. Oh, we know, we know, how hard it is to seize the road! Let the meek Christians repent for their sins in caves – we do what we need to do, and the new world – will be ours! Let our would-be "brother"-predator lust after the national wealth, let him incite the cities and entice the villages to follow him – we do what we need to do, and the new world – will be ours! Oh, we know, we know, how hard it is to seize the roads! When will you step out onto the right path, Ukraine? And you, my Dnipro-invalid, will you ever awaken, stubborn one?

V

You've turned gray, my Dnipro. Once wide – you've now grown narrow.[112] Oh, where is your spirit? Where is your ardor and your strength? You've surrounded yourself with bald spots along the shores: I'll flow, I'll run along the smooth bottom, I'll find magic kingdoms. Do you want peace and tranquility? Under whose hand? You've turned gray, my Dnipro. Once wide – you've now grown narrow.

Above you are storm clouds – armies of storm clouds! A furious wind swings sabers and screams: I'll hack whoever's not with us! I'll

---

112   The Dnipro is an extraordinarily wide river. The line echoes a famous poem by Taras Shevchenko, in which he writes: "Reve ta stohne Dnipr shyrokyi" (The wide Dnipro roars and moans).

chop you in two! And you: to the rapids I flow. Do you want peace and tranquility? Under whose hand? Certainly we already have a hand – it's strong and magnificent. And the sea waits and peers out. For everyone, for everyone, for everyone...

VI

Do you want me, Dnipro, to read for you? Once upon a time Ukraine raged!.. From border to border, from the Dniester River to the Danube, all the way to the sea and near Starodub – the rabble grabbed the gentry by the hair. (A red – sun – in the boundless – steppes...) Do you want me, Dnipro, to read for you?

And the gentry turned to popes, to kings, and the gentry built themselves a country. Oh, how many arose there! Oh, how many have lain down... Once upon a time Ukraine raged. The Dnipro smiled: you can read on – or not...

A red – sun – in the boundless – steppes.

VII

A gale from the north and south, from the west and east. Where to escape? Where to hide from the wind? Pillars of sand were lifted, in wisps they shimmered from a cliff... Dnipro! the storms are upon us! – Like a bear it rises – it splashes onto the shore with a single paw! the other is beneath the water...

Wake up, old one, wake up, the Rhine, the Volga, and the Dniester arose long ago, and the people have established a new order on your shores. A gale from the north and south, from the west and east. Come on, everyone let's join hands, hey, hey!

Pillars of sand rose, in wisps they shimmered from the cliff...

VIII

It dances to its heart's content somewhere else, but here it's still concealed. It flashes, it pings along iron rails, and for a long time it glides and hums. (It's raining...)

If only more, if only more often! Let the whole land pass through a storm! – It dances to its heart's content somewhere, but here it's still concealed.

Old men were knocking ashes out of their pipes, and we rake them into pyramids. – Puff away, mighty one, carry it off, blow it away, so that they never gather it up again. It flashes, it rumbles through iron, and for a long time it glides and hums.

It's raining...

IX

Sometimes – he's like a gentleman. All in blue, with white shores for stockings. "I'm going to a congress, to a congress." And he pretends that he's running, and believes that he's busy and preoccupied. All in blue, with white shores for stockings.

"Oh, have pity on us!" – both sides of the fields shout. "send us fog, for storm clouds are over the rich man's forests all the time." "I'm going to a congress, to a congress" – carelessly the Dnipro tosses back to them. "I'll protect you all, just leave me alone."

And suddenly— he turns back. He churns the foam on the waves and lies down, as he has lain down for centuries.
Sometimes – he's like a gentleman.[113]

---

113   A note in Pavlo Tychyna, *Zibrannia tvoriv v 12-y tomakh*, I, (Kyiv: Naukova dumka, 1983): 631 remarks that the "gentleman" of this poem is an allegorical figure of the Ukrainian free government's Central Rada.

X

We live as a commune, we work. All around us, a forest, lonely villages and people, wild as sweet-briar. Ah, so much joy, when you love the earth, when you seek harmony in life! For every one of us builds an altar to humanity, everyone is like an apostle. Ah, so much joy, when you love the earth. There are no angels, no God, no seven heavens. There's only pride and fervor, common work and praise.

Well what of it that blood has flooded the universe? Future generations will arise – the union of bodies and souls.

We do what we do, and the new world – it will be ours!

1920 Mezhhirya

BLACKSMITH STREET[114]

SUNSET I

I walk on, forward.
Somewhere, there, behind me is the sunset.
It threw its feverishly-yellow bullet onto the villages.
and waits...
And there are fumes and smoke,
and rooks above the cemetery...
I walk on, forward.
There, where the rails run parallel without end,
where sleepy dusk fades and grows dense.
And the final glance of the evening spins a web
    on reflecting windows, on towers, on churches.
Cataracts of dove-colored puddles
reflect the crimson tops of poplars
and in half-closed ripples cower from the wind.
And wind carries the dust, swings posters and at bazaars
    shakes up signboards the way a bandit shakes a city dweller...
The city very nearly falls asleep, swoons, forever growing mute.
no bread, no water, no friendly courtesy.
They carried off a corpse.
Sidewalks picked up their purses and dispersed.
And suddenly before me
with a gruff luster it became alive.
Blood boiled, and a brain splattered onto a fence.
And my shadow, like the shadow of a titan,
fell the length of the street heading somewhere...
And it became horrifying, just like at a great fire!
Be damned! It's you who bloomed so sweetly,
so that now we have only corpses, corpses and blood!
Will it not be the last time you play?

Somewhere, there, behind me is the sunset...

1921

---

114   My translation is a literal translation of *Kuznechna vulytsia*. Tychyna had an apartment on the street during his student days in Kyiv.

SUNSET II

No, I can't resist, I'll look back –
the west[115] is like a tilled volcanic field!
It's because Barbusse[116] is there,
because Rolland[117] is there.

I'll look back – the entire earth
is an ocean of blazes!
It's because, there, just as I do,
they cast their own shadow.

The shadow titans itself to the east,
I grow, I rise,
I proffer my hand to the strong
across the nation and my kin.

Above the heads of tribes
I saw you.
Oh, time
is blessed!

1921

---

115   Tychyna is playing on the dual meanings of the words *zakhid* (west or sunset) and *skhid* (east or sunrise).

116   Henri Barbusse (1873-1935). French realist novelist and journalist, as well as an early supporter of the Bolsheviks. His early works were anti-war novels that focused on soldiers as pawns enslaved to the upper classes. His later works are imbued with pro-communist politics. Tychyna, who spoke French, escorted him on a visit to Kharkiv in 1927. He met with him several times in subsequent years. Barbusse died in Moscow in 1935.

117   Romain Rolland (1866-1944). French novelist, dramatist, and biographer, who won the Nobel Prize for Literature in 1916. He was an ardent supporter of the Bolshevik revolution and organized the Paris Conference in Defense of Culture in 1935, which Tychyna attended. He had a greater reputation as a writer outside his own country. He advocated Buddhism as a means for resolving all the ills of the world.

THE SUN GREW FEEBLE...

The sun grew feeble. A hot violet color burns
on the buildings.
The last ray of light, like a stiletto,
stabbed the maple tree for autumn. A woman
takes down the wash. Around her
the wind swirled
and to its own tune began twirling dust around
her pink legs and full neck...
Just like in Hellas! The wind from the sea
puffs up the front of her blouse... What beauty!
And suddenly a quarrel: are you stealing? from despair? –
They're pulling each other's hair... The maple tree expires
and heals, then becomes tarnished.
The children play a game of war.
And – a dog is with them,
the "patriot" of his yard... So the day
ends. Above the city the din seethes.
The thin frost takes on all kinds of tones.
Only the mad steam engines
continuously whoop for someone every minute.
Let there be movement! Hearts! Wisdom![118]
Let there even be ferocious battle! –
Only in this way can the human being
and the entire material of life renew itself.

1920

EASTER SUNDAY

I walk back along Blacksmith Street. The sun
is just barely visible. This way: like a shadow
touched with a brush. The poplar is much redder!..

---

118   From the expression: "bude znattia, ta ne bude vorottia" (one will learn by experience, but it will be too late). The Pennsylvania German saying "Too old we get too shmart" might be a good equivalent.

They're still breaking their fast, there still is silence,
such laziness over everything!

Thin ice. Jackdaws have grown hoarse overnight,
but all the same... Behind them, everywhere, there's chirping,
somewhere there's a pigeon in echoing niches...
They're still breaking their fast, there still is silence,
such laziness over everything!

Why do I hear the peal?
Why is there boldness in me?
What kind of flotilla
from the unconquerable heights
develops such furious speed?

Where is the bell from?
And from where in my breast is this boundless feeling?
It's not Easter Sunday or Christmas.
a new, modern, solemn feast
is stirring and approaching.

And when it gets close and falls.
many of us will be blinded.
Such is the light there,
such is the flight of thought there.
that many of us will go blind.

Not that we are too old,
but just because it's too hard
to trust the grandiose,
to accept such a large dose
of paganism.

How blinding is the sun! The green sky
is so blue. What a day!
It's already daytime, and we still are in the churches,
and then we'll break our fasts in our burrows
and will sing our songs.

It's already completely daytime!

1921

THE FIRST OF MAY ON EASTER

Easter rain
along the sidewalk sil-
    ky verdure
sprouted from beneath the earth.

This is Christ who is risen
to quietly raise the dead
    the wind quietly maplebowed
the day.

Suddenly right here! suddenly!
an orchestra broke through:
it's not Christ who is risen –
but the Working Class.

Suddenly right here! suddenly!
a procession of workers
    is there a redder
holiday than this May?

It thundered, it rang out,
with a stamping it started off the
    day maplebowed
the silky verdure.

1921

KHARKIV

I

Kharkiv, Kharkiv, where is your countenance?
for whom is your call?
You've sunken in the clay of many rivers,
dark as the night.

You've sunken this way: between the hills
You're stamping in one spot.
And suddenly you break through the bridges –
and already You're in the steppe!

And already the wind is whipping you –
in chase, chase and pursuit!..
Hey! son of a gun,
here you've become unstoppable –

Here (just as the dawn flashes) –
what city center shout could match it! –
you hum and hum, and you'll gush in a chord.
until the workingman comes.

You hum, hum... and when you burn out,
for a long time then, for a long time it echoes...
And it seems: somewhere... there... The Donbas whistle
answers you in tune.

They answer from the fog of the land beyond the river:
axes, saws, and a metallic ring...
That, Kharkiv, is your countenance,
here is your center.

1923

II

The streets roll past, the pavement clicks with hooves in darkness.
The marshy snow. The March marshy rain.
Just above a clock is glowing over you,
over your and over our head.

The streets roll past, a tram car runs across the abyss.
Land of the steppe! Oh, what an untamed land!
Just above it's glowing over you,
over your and over our head.

Land of the steppe! Oh, how wild and violent is the wind!
When it strikes – it tears telephone wires, twists them into bunches!
And for a long time it resounds above you,
over your and over our head.

Far off through the ravines are misery and typhus.
                        Bushes beyond bushes...
Who is this beneath a shop window madly sniveling in the rain? –
A responsibility hangs above you,
over your and over our head.

Above your spring there is still such wind and darkness!
Here you leap across – there is no way out.
There you will stand – as though You're really in the capital:
roof crowds upon roof, the streets roll past...

The streets roll past, the pavement clicks with hooves in darkness.
The marshy-snow. The March marshy rain.
Just above a clock is glowing over you,
over your and over our head.

1923

A FUGUE

I pass through the cemetery.
Summer is still sitting at its plentiful table,
the day still wears an open collar,
but something in nature is sobbing.

Sway, terraces of trees, –
today You're in such pain!..

> The wind, the wind whips
> tormenting an oak a maple
> a somber dream on clouds
> again this is an autumn wind[119]

Summer is still sitting at its plentiful table,
But there's already jaundice in the leaves.
Growing yellow.
To sleep.
First here, then there.
throughout the entire cemetery.
A beautiful dream! A terraced dream!
But where is the meaning in it? What is its aim?
Who dreams it? from where does it come?
                                       (Ai! Ai-ye!)

Or perhaps only the dead see in their dreams? –
blood?
and battle?

If only once to hear that language,
with which the other world believes!
O no, the other world will not dawn.
 Only an echo once in a while... muddled... reaches us.
a-ye... A-ye...

---

[119] Tychyna divides several of the words in this strophe across line boundaries, which is difficult if not impossible to convey in translation.

> The wind will call out
> bending an oak maple
> a somber dream on clouds
> again this is an autumn wind

The hillocks have lain down in arches.
Graves, like piglets, have swollen,
and above them
crosses.
In torn shirts, in worker's jackets,
after a sleepless night, they run and fall,
and they become entangled in a leaf, like in factory whistles.
And following them
black monuments reflect scornful laughter with their mirror-eyes:
"The last thing one needs here is you!"

> "Yes, yes, right here!
> We're from under the yoke, out of prison!
> The liberating wind is with
>   us."

I listen closely:
I bear within myself
a voice that grows fuller.
The living – long ago have diffused into cells,
a cell – into the earth, into the verdure, into the rustling.
And all that protest, that fire that they had,
now has become the verdure and the rustling.

> Resound, resound, lush treetops,
> oh, windy epoch of ours!
> Pass through from the old cemetery,
> oh, melody of mine.

Wherever I go – a semicircle.
Wherever I stand – an oval!
The clouds arched their backs.
Leaves wheel along the road.

.and the entire azure sail
carries my round soul
on oars into eternity –
    –oh, melody of mine –

So what is the matter, heart? You're lamenting, crying?
That we're incapable of embracing the world,
not even a fraction of it?
                    (the wind whips)
Is it not so, my love? A river of thought
and radio currents, like a frenzied hand,
will opendoor[120] the universe. And there will be no lock.
                    (the wind calls)
Is it no so, my darling?
Yes, yes, the misery and sloth will disappear.
The enmity of nations, too.
and the boundaries of planets will push open,
and we will repeat our circle
in our constant growth
toward eternity!...
And all the same it will not always be clear:
the verdure... the rustling...
    "The rustling – it's unclear, isn't it?"
    this blood, and the destruction of the old...
    A creaky voice from the grave
    was carried to me by the wind in a stream.

"Unclear, right, it's unclear?"
And I see, another one awakens:
your heart has awakened me,
that sensitive heart of yours.

    Oh, brother, call out the graveyard!
    Look at all that blackness!

---

120   Tychyna creates a neologism here *rozdveriat'*, which is composed of the prefix *roz-* meaning movement in several directions and the noun *dveri* (door) with a verbal ending.

> We'll strike to the east together,
> and the west will extend us a hand.
>
> And old men already are there to help,
> a great quantity of landowners, of offertory priests...
> Just think, we'd be living once again
> if only you would lead us.

I look – the specters come again...
I fly downward from a hillock, I run!
And opposite me is a withered sun,
And the wind cuts scabs upon scabs...

And the wind hurls scabs upon scabs
into my eyes, my soul, my breast, my mouth...
Where are you rushing to, madman?
Stop! Damn you!

I listen closely:
I bear within myself
a voice that grows fuller.
The living – long ago have diffused into cells,
a cell – into the earth, into the verdure, into the rustling.
And all that protest, that fire that they had,
now has become the verdure and the rustling.

> Resound, resound, lush treetops,
> o, windy epoch of ours!
> Pass through from the old cemetery,
> o, melody of mine.

The clouds arched their backs. The hilltops bent.
And who reflects whom – I don't know, I don't.
Only all this stirs and speaks,
and swings the prematurely born verdure and gold and blood,
blood...
And in this stirring,
like the quick fingering of a harp in an orchestra –

the quivering of aspen leaves.
And in this stirring, just before dawn somewhere,
is the apron of a birch.
And unexpectedly
a bird...
And all this swings, and stirs, and speaks.

1921

OTHER POEMS

IN MEMORY OF THE THIRTY

On Askold's Hill
They buried them –
Thirty daring Ukrainian men,
Magnificent and young...
On Askold's Hill
The flower of Ukraine! –
We go into the world
Along a bloody road.
Whose traitorous hand
Dared rise against whom? –
The sun blossoms, the wind plays,
And the River Dnipro...
Against whom did Cain set himself?
Lord, avenge them! –
More than anything they loved
Their beloved land.
They died in a New Testament
With the glory of saints. –
At Askold's Hill
They buried them.

March 8 (21) 1918

MOTHER WAS PEALING POTATOES...

Mother was pealing potatoes and her two baby girls playing with dolls.
They all were sitting on the floor thinking their own thoughts.
Mother: how will they be able to live now? Will they at least parcel out the field
to us?
and even if they parcel it out from that patch? We'll starve anyway,
there will be sorrow and tears! Maybe my son can hire himself out and
                              help some.
They've already endured so much, suffered enough, how will it be
                              from now on –
who knows... The little girls followed her, then sat down deftly,
They taught the dolls to hoe in the garden: this way and that way, see,
you need to do it like this; not only the surface but also stir it underneath –
This way it'll grow the way it should and bear fruit
                              so that all of us and mother
will have enough by winter. Mother heard this and turned to them:
My little swallows, my sweet little birdies!.. She wanted to say
something else, but she couldn't. Her tears, burning on
                              her eyelashes
fell on her hand that lay on her knee (a knife fell out
inconspicuously), her other hand was still quietly holding
the potato: it was trembling, and the rings of potato skin quivered,
not quite pealed off they hung down tenuously from the potatoes ...
The children grew quiet, left their dolls and joined her in crying.
The mother grabbed them, hugged them with her arm,
                              and with her other
wiped away their tears. The potato peal broke off, and falling, rolled up
                              on the doll
like a serpent...
    Here her son enters: "Mom! Are you at it again? If
you could just stop crying, it might be easier!
Do you hear me, Mom?"
She put those potatoes on the stove. Getting the pot grabber,
she took hold of the iron pot from below and pushed
                              it deeper to the left,
where the swirl began burning, a swirl as though from a fiery

            wire –
the firewood started to crackle. "Yes, I can hear,
           I'm not completely deaf!"
The firewood began to crackle, and a dark blue cloud
             was menacing in the windows.
The sisters looked harshly and moved away from the stove.
("Maybe I'm not totally deaf yet"). A dark blue cloud was menacing in
             the windows...
  The son stood for awhile there, and then began
 to pace around the house:
"Father hasn't returned yet?" Mother said as if thinking aloud:
You see, I'm already old, and stupid, and useless. Do I know anything?
What's left for me to do other than cry? My son is a communist,
         his father
gone mad, he foolishly joined the shtundists,[121] if only he had done just
           that –
But he calls himself Jesus Christ, leads his party throughout the villages!
Tell me then what's left? So slash, so
          thrash,
crush me in a coffin with the little children, let me be
strangled by your knee like Ukraine."
   Her son laughed! Well, what's this about? Why
such talk?
    You just stand up for your Ukraine
    And leave me alone.
I'm not little anymore and know what I'm doing.
If you want – I'll live alone without you,
           completely.
Tomorrow, no today I'll leave and won't come back. I already know
           where I'll go!
Mother grew silent, sharpened her knife scratching the iron pot.
The children from under the table rolled out a pumpkin

---

121 Shtundists were a sect of dissenting Ukrainian peasants founded circa 1860. Their group based their beliefs on Baptist practices of daily hourly Bible readings and rejection of central church authority. The name of their sect comes from the German word *Stunde*, which means "hour," referring to the hourly Bible study.

                              for her and shouted: Let's go:
You see him listen, a little bull with a single horn bald on his forehead!
Let's go! And her son said a little softer: as you wish, I'll go and not
                              come back.
"What do I want there! To stab myself with the knife
so as not to see this misery – that's what
                                        I want!"
The pumpkin split with a thud and broke in
                              two.
In the house it smelled of walnut seeds and a little bit of frost.
The children stooped over to take a bite of their half – they banged
                              their little
heads. It became funny for them! So, taking out the innards,
they started to giggle, bursting into laughter. Each
looks at the other, and again, until a hiccup attack.
"But we'll have to do something
                    with father."
Her son: I know what you are saying.
(A pause. The cat jumped down from shelf above the oven).
                              Though he won't repent. Hardly.
Something clanked in the hallway, banged into the door.
                              "Oh, mommy, I'm afraid!
The children to their mother: Mommy, I'm afraid he's going to beat us!"
The door opened wide from momentum, and something
                              shouted from there:
"Fall to the floor: Christ has appeared! Greet him, sing,
Beat the cymbals, the tambourines: Christ your God and king has
                              appeared!
Silence reigned. The iron kettle hissed. Menacingly dark blue –
                              silence – in the windows –
   Blessing to the right and left, God entered
   the house: wearing a shirt under a belt,
   barefoot, a narrow forehead two fingers wide.
God: I've grown weary! I'll sit down, sit for a while. What are you
cooking there?
You know, today I rose up into heaven and I felt such pity,
   Such pity for you. The apostles say: "Jump up,
                              hosanna!

I wave my arms, flying higher and I higher, I wave again,
                              going higher and higher.
Mother: You satan's spawn, you foul creature, why are you
coming to me? You've brought us misery, abandoned the children –
go back from where you came, and don't look at the stove, Judas!
Why did you throw the door wide open? You hear, drunken bastard?
God: If you don't believe – touch my immaculate ribs.
Do you see the nail wounds in my hands? – I was crucified
                              for you.
Mother: Go away, because if I by God take that pot grabber, it will be
to your ribs, your head and hands – do you hear me?
Her son (spitting through his teeth on the floor): This is pure
theeater performance.

Lenin the antichrist appeared, my son, and you talk about theeaters.
We must do battle: the antichrist appeared.

And you first make an appearance before the town council, and then
we'll talk about the antichrist. There... they say...
And, well, the devil take it – some day you'll
get yours!

Lenin the antichrist appeared, my son, but you are against me.
We must do battle: the enemy appeared.

The neighbor girl at the door: O, auntie,
have you heard? Larivon the shtundist killed
his youngest daughter!

Her son. Reluctantly. He turned around – blood for blood! Right
opposite him eyebrows stood up
Jesus Christ rose up.
And mother began to sob.

1926

THE FUNERAL OF MY FRIEND

Already sadly the evening changed its color from
crimson to a grayish-violet.
I shoveled the blue snow from the house
and stopped... A deep blue orchestral
lament flowed into me. It wept
and choked on the dry frost:
and fell green to the firs
that reddened above by the road,
then echoed mutely somewhere in the garden.
And it wafted from the moon in the breeze,
like a tone not built on harmony,
there thousands of orchestras played together,
mixing motifs...
Everything changes, becomes renewed, hurries, bleeds blood in wounds,
beats the breast
out of sadness, becomes clogged with silt, becomes dust, passes along
all of itself
to the damp earth.
Over whom did those *surmas*[122] weep?
Why did the cymbals clang?
And when the drum beats as though it were a chest—
whose lifetime had ended?
...The crimson color died out.
A cloud glistened
watery green. The world appeared opaque—
like an x-ray...
And I jumped up and began to run! It was just
this kind of evening two years ago
as I said good-bye to my friend. A fiery horse
then bolted off into the distance and disappeared... And the days
passed—the war struck. And I heard about
my friend: the entire country
was proud of him, he, who like a plow
had driven into the enemy! And serpent's blood

---

122   See note #65.

rose around him up to his knees...
And my friend Yaroslav, even after that
was often on everyone's lips. There was
a vicious battle for Kharkiv. Our guys surrounded it with determination.
All the same
it wasn't an even battle, and Yaroslav
was forced to fight all night in the glow of fires
against eight of the enemy. He deserved
even more glory when he saved people whom the Nazis had planned
to hang. He fought with the army to take back a village,
and he died there... His death is teaching me
to grow angry, incredibly angry! I heard about you, my friend,
on the radio—and suddenly in my eyes your casket
began to loom... I wanted so—
to see you in your casket at least!

Everything changes, becomes renewed, hurries...
...And before me
your catalfaque swayed as though in a dream.
On reaching the procession, I looked
into the closed casket, though I knew well
that Yaroslav was not here: they're burying him
without me... there... at the front! And the orchestra
began to sob again.
Everything changes, becomes renewed, hurries,
Everything passes into new forms in the world.
And it's strange! The *surmas* are playing,
soldiers are marching in procession, and I
(in no way can I rid myself of my split feelings)
watch as a beet-colored stream
disappears at sunset... And I'm not interested –
Over whom were the *surmas* weeping?
Or why did the cymbals clang?
And when the drum beat as though it were a chest—
whose lifetime had ended?
Whom then—do I need to ask?
there is a warrior in this casket—that means one who defended
freedom, freedom in our land! It began

to dawn over the entire world from us. Along just such a field
a flower has bloomed—
of brotherhood and friendship... the star of Slavdom
already has shone on the West!.. And here—out of time
the yowling of Nazi butchery began,
It sharpened its claws—and wounded us all
sparing no one... The orchestra is playing
somberly, but it seems to me: this is a lament
from Ukraine... Let the *surmas* sob!
Let them unleash the grief of the widow and mother,
who walk behind the casket, they grieve
and weep—stretching out their hands... You!
Thrice-damned Nazis! You will never
conquer us! Why are you
torturing innocent people? Because
you're superior? More noble? It's all a lie!
Nobility doesn't help a dog—
much less a wolf.
...As though it were a wolf on its paws—
in the west a cloud bared its teeth.
Dusk fell. The orchestra grew silent,
and it became quiet... The Wolf Company
passed through the mill to meet us. They had transported
linen to the military hospital on sleds. Children
passed by with a dog. In a hoarse tone
the factory whistled and grew quiet. It was about to turn dark.
And the city changed before our eyes. The snow
on the street shone like phosphorous.
From the lantern of the procession a shaft of a ray
kept shining ahead... Sadness lay upon me—
and my soul sang a requiem with the choir.
Everything changes, becomes renewed, hurries,
bleeds blood in wounds, out of sadness
beats the breast, becomes clogged up with silt, becomes dust,
passes along all of itself to the damp earth.
Everything passes into new forms in the world, abides in darkness—and
on the sun as though in paradise. From land to land a person wanders
across the entire world in order to lay out their eternity again.

And every day, and every clear hour
the earth splits open and closes.
And it grinds a person in its teeth
like a chance serpent of chaos.

But no, life holds a strict progression,
And what appears to be chaos is delicate harmony.
Look at history: a readiness to do battle
illuminates you with all its faceted mirrors.

A readiness to stand up in battle for your freedom
for oppressed nations and the disenfranchised slave.
You will not attain immortality if you find no place
to ford across the battle of truth.

And the earth itself is not a serpent, but your mother,
who always carries and caresses you…
No one can break the laws of battle,
No one can change the laws of motherhood.

And the fact that movement in the world happens in leaps and bounds,
   not smoothly,
Tell us: Go! Only our path is true!
You drink blood, you fascist Nazi blood suckers!
You'll get yours—don't worry!—you won't be given
any water!

And you'll croak without water. Your people will remain
Who will, if not itself a slave, will awaken to
                                                      battle.
Everything changes, becomes renewed, hurries,
Moves to a bright populist era.
You are accustomed to stealing—like a robber.
And you'll end up plucked like a bird.
Everything changes, grows moldy, becomes rumpled,
like creative clay in the hands of a sculptor.
But the sculptor is the nation itself that stands,
does not bend,

though you rush to make him your slave.
Everything rises, awakens, grows and laughs,
And you, the dead one—cannot kill us the living.
...The orchestra began to play. Our entire procession
turned into an alley—
and the fires of the factory flashed... Up to the skies
it somehow became higher: the bright muzzles
of the projectors cut all the way
to the skies—and began to shift...

The slabs, like tassels of banners,
scraps of needles from snow-covered pines
hung down...
Everything changes, becomes renewed, hurries,
bleeds blood in wounds, beats the breast
out of its sadness, becomes clogged up with silt, becomes dust,
then rises again from beneath the earth.
Ah! We're already at the cemetery.
They halted the horses. Took the casket
in their hands gingerly. (Like sugar-coated candy—
powdery snow sprinkled from the trees and snowily
rolled down from my eyelid). I grasped the casket
to put it on my shoulder. We carried it,
and everyone caught up to us (because life
rushes)—one with heavy ropes,
one with a shovel. And each sank
in the snow—as all of us were sinking. All the same
we made our way somehow through the crosses. The frost
had settled in for the night. With our sacred burden
we made our way to the grave and, taking the casket
from our shoulders, we placed it on the clay
that had come off from the edges.
"The red sword!"
An orator blared, "protects the whole country
From the Nazis!" (A neighboring meadow
Suddenly began to rustle. A woman fell with a shout:
"Open up the casket!... Son, give me your hand!
Oh, what did my child ever do to you?"

...And a second followed after her—but not with lament,
But with the howling of sobbing: "Wake up,
Stepan, wake up!") "With this sword!"
The speaker said again, "you should
Slash off the Teuton's head! All our equipment
Rises to battle, all our living forces.
A partisan shakes our hand
From Yugolsavia! Insurrectionists have already
begun to ring to the examination of those
sacred knives in Poland! Bachka, Transcarpathia
is seething!.. The anger of the people in no way has quieted
even in the Czech lands! There more than one tyrant
has scattered into rags... Brothers! He, who defended
his homeland will live in the
centuries!"
The orator quieted for a moment,
pointed to the casket and said: "Stepan
has been tortured for Ukraine... you'd hardly recognize him.
And here – he's been brought home."
(At those words his wife and mother again
began to sob. We stood in the nighttime
gloom like shadows. The silent
frost thoroughly burned our soul!) "Heroes
know no fear! Their bright deed
calls us: Against the enemy! To our weapons!"

...Here a volley thundered. It kicked up
as if a storm touched all with its wing.
And crying, shouting, and moaning!.. And something
heavy floated into the earth... And the grave
swallowed him. And they began to sprinkle clods
of earth on him. And the coffin hollowly
droned. And shouts were mixed
with the sobbing of the orchestra. A single star
twinkled in the sky...

And the *surmas* sadly wept.
The cymbals clanged resoundingly.

And the drum beat as though inside a chest:
you ended your life in glory.
... And I cried myself out!
I don't know: how and with whom I returned.
The entire earth shone in phosphorus...
And a requiem in my soul was being sung:
Everything changes, becomes renewed, hurries,
bleeds blood in wounds, beats the breast
out of its sadness, becomes clogged up with silt, becomes dust,
then rises again green from beneath the earth.
And when I returned home: in the courtyard
my shovel was still sticking out in the snow.
The dark
silence was oh so bitter. Just up high
a greenish
star twinkled...
Twinkle, shine and beam! We'll wait until
we bury all the beasts in a cramped grave
with our spade! Here-here
we'll overthrow their force...

Everything rises, awakens, grows and laughs.

We will fight for we are alive!
And we will not stop avenging the enemy!
Until we step on the Nazi head
with our foot.

Though it is difficult for us,
though our wounds are painful –
we will not let the enemies
engorge themselves on us!

I didn't speak to anyone in the house:
I threw myself onto the hard bed to fall asleep.
...And your catalfaque swayed in my eyes,

and you could hear –
Everything rises, awakens, grows and laughs.
and you could hear –
Everything passes into new forms in the world.
And you, the dead one—cannot kill us the living.

And it was as if Stepan had gotten up and was walking,
and Yaroslav was with him. It's spring! Azure blue!
Tractors are riding into the field. And a singing lark
howls. And the young
generation is flying here on horses
from behind the mountain. And he, who is leading them,
speaks: "We are borrowing
your knowledge from you now –
to fight the enemy! The nation ached
in suffering, in grief. But the nation has not died –
we will defeat the fascists, we will!"
And it was as if all, having drank the water
that Yaroslav's and Stepan's mother
had carried out to them, they closed their ranks
and flew off into battle. And glory
accompanied them – up, up
in airplanes...

And here suddenly
I awakened Oh, it's already dark! Night.
The predatory hand of the snowstorm knocked
on the old, thin walls. The snow rustled
along the pane... Oh, what is that? Where am I?
Suddenly I remembered everything. And already
I couldn't keep my eyelids shut. The powerful idea
of freedom and the justice of life
lifted me like a child in one's arms,
and everything became visible, as if in the palm of my hand.
We will go on living – both you and I!
We'll wind around like ivy along that column.
We'll rebuild the cities, we'll plant
the gardens, we'll lift up individuality.

So be gone now, spirit of the fascist horde!
Be gone and don't stain the conscience of a person!

Why have you stood up, damned one, on the path?
What is the reason for the satanic arena
of your humiliations? You are dead in life!
You're already dead!
And frightfully in the darkness
a blizzard began to howl like that siren...
After listening for a minute, I lay down again.
And I so wanted to go to the Dnipro-Slavuta![123]
Snow rustled along the pane...
And I could hear –
the *surmas* weeping somewhere there,
the cymbals quietly clanged,
and a drum continued to hollowly beat:
– In glory you –
ended
your life...

1942

---

123   The Dnipro River in the past has also been called the Slavuta or Slavutych, the river of Slavs.

CONTENTS

INTRODUCTION	5
ACKNOWLEDGMENTS	13
THE SENSES AND NONSENSES OF PAVLO TYCHYNA	15
CLARINETS OF THE SUN (1918)	20
NOT ZEUS, OR PAN, OR THE DOVE-SPIRIT...	20
THE CLOUDS SWIRLED INTO CURLS...	21
GROVES RUSTLE	22
LIKE HARPS, LIKE HARPS	23
SOMEWHERE SPRING APPROACHED...	24
THE FLOWER IN MY HEART...	25
DON'T LOOK SO FONDLY...	26
SHE LOOKED AT ME BRIGHTLY...	27
I CRIED FROM LOVE, I SOBBED...	28
O MISS INNA...	29
I'M STANDING AT THE BEND...	30
THE POPLARS IN THE FALLOW FIELD ARE FREE...	31
A GIRL'S EMBROIDERING...	32
A FLOWERY MEADOW...	33
O NATURE, DON'T CONCEAL...	34
THE BIRDS ARE STILL...	35
IT'S DAWNING...	36
ENHARMONIES	37
THEY TRAMPLE FLOWERS...	39
TO THE CATHEDRAL	40
PASTELS	42

I WENT TO THE GROVE…	44
SOMEONE WAS CARESSING THE FIELDS…	45
ON STEEP CLIFFS…	46
A CHILD WENT OUT FOR BREAD…	48
OPEN THE DOOR…	49
SORROWFUL MOTHER	50
ALONG THE AZURE STEPPE…	53
LULLABY	54
THE CHOIR OF BELL-FLOWERS	56
GREEN SUNDAY	58
WAR	59
A *DUMA* ON THREE WINDS	61
THE GOLDEN HUM	64

THE PLOW (1920) … 71

THE PLOW	72
SOW SEEDS…	73
AND BELY AND BLOK…	74
ON THE SQUARE…	76
HE FELL…	77
THEY OUTSTAR THE STARS…	78
IT WILL BE THIS WAY…	79
INTERPLANETARY INTERVALS…	80
JUST BEYOND THE VILLAGE…	81
AT SHEVCHENKO'S GRAVE…	82
THE MESSIAH	86
FROM THE CYCLE "CREATION OF THE WORLD"	87
LETTERS TO A POET	89
MADONNA OF MINE…	91
A PSALM TO IRON	94
RONDELS	97

I KNOW…	100
FOR HNAT MYKHAILYCHENKO	101
ONE ESCAPED IN LOVE…	102
FOR SHRIVELLED PROPHETS	103
BURN THE PROCLAMATIONS…	104

INSTEAD OF SONNETS AND OCTAVES (1920) 105

INSTEAD OF SONNETS AND OCTAVES	106

IN THE ORCHESTRA OF THE COSMOS (1921) 118

IN THE ORCHESTRA OF THE COSMOS	118

WIND FROM UKRAINE (1924) 129

WIND FROM UKRAINE	130
YAROSLAVNA'S LAMENT	132
SUMMER'S ON THE WAY…	136
MYKYTA THE TANNER	138
THREE SONS	140
FAUST IS WALKING…	142
FAMINE	143
AN ANSWER TO MY COUNTRYMEN	144
I WILL SPEAK FOR ALL…	146
O STRENGTH OF MY HATE…	148
TO GREAT LIARS	150
BEFORE A MONUMENT TO PUSHKIN IN ODESSA	151
SUCH A LOVELY AUTUMN…	152
ON A FARMSTEAD	153
WE SAY…	154
SPRING	155
LA BELLA FORNARINA	157
STORM CLOUDS LAY ALL AROUND…	158
THE REBELS	159
CLEON AND DIODOT	162

FROM MY DIARY	165
WE LIVE AS A COMMUNE	167
BLACKSMITH STREET	172
KHARKIV	177
A FUGUE	179
OTHER POEMS	186
IN MEMORY OF THE THIRTY	186
MOTHER WAS PEALING POTATOES...	187
THE FUNERAL OF MY FRIEND	191

Glagoslav Publications Catalogue

- *The Time of Women* by Elena Chizhova
- *Andrei Tarkovsky: A Life on the Cross* by Lyudmila Boyadzhieva
- *Sin* by Zakhar Prilepin
- *Hardly Ever Otherwise* by Maria Matios
- *Khatyn* by Ales Adamovich
- *The Lost Button* by Irene Rozdobudko
- *Christened with Crosses* by Eduard Kochergin
- *The Vital Needs of the Dead* by Igor Sakhnovsky
- *The Sarabande of Sara's Band* by Larysa Denysenko
- *A Poet and Bin Laden* by Hamid Ismailov
- *Zo Gaat Dat in Rusland* (Dutch Edition) by Maria Konjoekova
- *Kobzar* by Taras Shevchenko
- *The Stone Bridge* by Alexander Terekhov
- *Moryak* by Lee Mandel
- *King Stakh's Wild Hunt* by Uladzimir Karatkevich
- *The Hawks of Peace* by Dmitry Rogozin
- *Harlequin's Costume* by Leonid Yuzefovich
- *Depeche Mode* by Serhii Zhadan
- *Groot Slem en Andere Verhalen* (Dutch Edition) by Leonid Andrejev
- *METRO 2033* (Dutch Edition) by Dmitry Glukhovsky
- *METRO 2034* (Dutch Edition) by Dmitry Glukhovsky
- *A Russian Story* by Eugenia Kononenko
- *Herstories, An Anthology of New Ukrainian Women Prose Writers*
- *The Battle of the Sexes Russian Style* by Nadezhda Ptushkina
- *A Book Without Photographs* by Sergey Shargunov
- *Down Among The Fishes* by Natalka Babina
- *disUNITY* by Anatoly Kudryavitsky
- *Sankya* by Zakhar Prilepin
- *Wolf Messing* by Tatiana Lungin
- *Good Stalin* by Victor Erofeyev
- *Solar Plexus* by Rustam Ibragimbekov
- *Don't Call me a Victim!* by Dina Yafasova
- *Poetin* (Dutch Edition) by Chris Hutchins and Alexander Korobko

- *A History of Belarus* by Lubov Bazan
- *Children's Fashion of the Russian Empire* by Alexander Vasiliev
- *Empire of Corruption: The Russian National Pastime* by Vladimir Soloviev
- *Heroes of the 90s: People and Money. The Modern History of Russian Capitalism* by Alexander Solovev, Vladislav Dorofeev and Valeria Bashkirova
- *Fifty Highlights from the Russian Literature* (Dutch Edition) by Maarten Tengbergen
- *Bajesvolk* (Dutch Edition) by Michail Chodorkovsky
- *Dagboek van Keizerin Alexandra* (Dutch Edition)
- *Myths about Russia* by Vladimir Medinskiy
- *Boris Yeltsin: The Decade that Shook the World* by Boris Minaev
- *A Man Of Change: A study of the political life of Boris Yeltsin*
- *Sberbank: The Rebirth of Russia's Financial Giant* by Evgeny Karasyuk
- *To Get Ukraine* by Oleksandr Shyshko
- *Asystole* by Oleg Pavlov
- *Gnedich* by Maria Rybakova
- *Marina Tsvetaeva: The Essential Poetry*
- *Multiple Personalities* by Tatyana Shcherbina
- *The Investigator* by Margarita Khemlin
- *The Exile* by Zinaida Tulub
- *Leo Tolstoy: Flight from Paradise* by Pavel Basinsky
- *Moscow in the 1930* by Natalia Gromova
- *Laurus* (Dutch edition) by Evgenij Vodolazkin
- *Prisoner* by Anna Nemzer
- *The Crime of Chernobyl: The Nuclear Goulag* by Wladimir Tchertkoff
- *Alpine Ballad* by Vasil Bykau
- *The Complete Correspondence of Hryhory Skovoroda*
- *The Tale of Aypi* by Ak Welsapar
- *Selected Poems* by Lydia Grigorieva
- *The Fantastic Worlds of Yuri Vynnychuk*
- *The Garden of Divine Songs and Collected Poetry of Hryhory Skovoroda*
- *Adventures in the Slavic Kitchen: A Book of Essays with Recipes* by Igor Klekh
- *Seven Signs of the Lion* by Michael M. Naydan

- *Forefathers' Eve* by Adam Mickiewicz
- *One-Two* by Igor Eliseev
- *Girls, be Good* by Bojan Babić
- *Time of the Octopus* by Anatoly Kucherena
- *The Grand Harmony* by Bohdan Ihor Antonych
- *The Selected Lyric Poetry Of Maksym Rylsky*
- *The Shining Light* by Galymkair Mutanov
- *The Frontier: 28 Contemporary Ukrainian Poets - An Anthology*
- *Acropolis: The Wawel Plays* by Stanisław Wyspiański
- *Contours of the City* by Attyla Mohylny
- *Conversations Before Silence: The Selected Poetry of Oles Ilchenko*
- *The Secret History of my Sojourn in Russia* by Jaroslav Hašek
- *Mirror Sand: An Anthology of Russian Short Poems*
- *Maybe We're Leaving* by Jan Balaban
- *Death of the Snake Catcher* by Ak Welsapar
- *A Brown Man in Russia* by Vijay Menon
- *Hard Times* by Ostap Vyshnia
- *The Flying Dutchman* by Anatoly Kudryavitsky
- *Nikolai Gumilev's Africa* by Nikolai Gumilev
- *Combustions* by Srđan Srdić
- *The Sonnets* by Adam Mickiewicz
- *Dramatic Works* by Zygmunt Krasiński
- *Four Plays* by Juliusz Słowacki
- *Little Zinnobers* by Elena Chizhova
- *We Are Building Capitalism! Moscow in Transition 1992-1997* by Robert Stephenson
- *The Nuremberg Trials* by Alexander Zvyagintsev
- *The Hemingway Game* by Evgeni Grishkovets
- *A Flame Out at Sea* by Dmitry Novikov
- *Jesus' Cat* by Grig
- *Want a Baby and Other Plays* by Sergei Tretyakov
- *Mikhail Bulgakov: The Life and Times* by Marietta Chudakova
- *Leonardo's Handwriting* by Dina Rubina
- *A Burglar of the Better Sort* by Tytus Czyżewski
- *The Mouseiad and other Mock Epics* by Ignacy Krasicki
- *Ravens before Noah* by Susanna Harutyunyan

- *An English Queen and Stalingrad* by Natalia Kulishenko
- *Point Zero* by Narek Malian
- *Absolute Zero* by Artem Chekh
- *Olanda* by Rafał Wojasiński
- *Robinsons* by Aram Pachyan
- *The Monastery* by Zakhar Prilepin
- *The Selected Poetry of Bohdan Rubchak: Songs of Love, Songs of Death, Songs of the Moon*
- *Mebet* by Alexander Grigorenko
- *The Orchestra* by Vladimir Gonik
- *Everyday Stories* by Mima Mihajlović
- *Slavdom* by Ľudovít Štúr
- *The Code of Civilization* by Vyacheslav Nikonov
- *Where Was the Angel Going?* by Jan Balaban
- *De Zwarte Kip* (Dutch Edition) by Antoni Pogorelski
- *Głosy / Voices* by Jan Polkowski
- *Sergei Tretyakov: A Revolutionary Writer in Stalin's Russia* by Robert Leach
- *Opstand* (Dutch Edition) by Władysław Reymont
- *Dramatic Works* by Cyprian Kamil Norwid
- *Children's First Book of Chess* by Natalie Shevando and Matthew McMillion
- *Precursor* by Vasyl Shevchuk
- *The Vow: A Requiem for the Fifties* by Jiří Kratochvil
- *De Bibliothecaris* (Dutch edition) by Mikhail Jelizarov
- *Subterranean Fire* by Natalka Bilotserkivets
- *Vladimir Vysotsky: Selected Works*
- *Behind the Silk Curtain* by Gulistan Khamzayeva
- *The Village Teacher and Other Stories* by Theodore Odrach
- *Duel* by Borys Antonenko-Davydovych
- *War Poems* by Alexander Korotko
- *Ballads and Romances* by Adam Mickiewicz
- *The Revolt of the Animals* by Wladyslaw Reymont
- *Liza's Waterfall: The hidden story of a Russian feminist* by Pavel Basinsky
- *Biography of Sergei Prokofiev* by Igor Vishnevetsky

More coming . . .

GLAGOSLAV PUBLICATIONS
www.glagoslav.com

www.ingramcontent.com/pod-product-compliance
Lightning Source LLC
Chambersburg PA
CBHW031108080526
44587CB00011B/880